A SPIRITUALITY OF WHOLENESS

THE *grace* NEW LOOK AT

BILL HUEBSCH

TWENTY-THIRD PUBLICATIONS
Mystic, Connecticut

Fourth printing 1992

Twenty-Third Publications
185 Willow Street
P.O. Box 180
Mystic, CT 06355
(203) 536-2611
800-321-0411

ISBN 0-89622-355-8
Library of Congress Catalog Card No. 87-51566

"Not since Louis Evely's *That Man Is You* have I come across a book so delightfully powerful....a great source for meditation as well as inspiration.

"For the perplexed Catholic who wonders what has happened to the faith that was learned in grade school; for the 'cafeteria Catholic' who since Vatican II has picked up bits of renewed Catholicism and would like to see how it fits into the bigger picture; for the serious student of contemporary theology who struggles with the 'big names' and wants to meditate on the marvels of it all; and for those who long for theology in the key of C—here is a book to read and re-read and then hand on to someone else. It's that kind of book."

Fr. Edmond Dunn
St. Ambrose University

"Bill Huebsch has written one of the few books I didn't want to end. It isn't easy to write about grace, nor is it very exciting to read about it, but with his style, turn-of-phrase, and sensitivity to the human condition, Huebsch helps us experience grace as we read his reflections. His context is contemporary living, his scriptural insights are creative, his suggestions to experience grace (the 'holy pause') are concrete and do-able ('holy sharing'), and his humor regularly rises to make the book all the more enjoyable."

Michael H. Crosby, OFMCap.
author of *Spirituality of the Beatitudes*

"Huebsch has looked with the eyes of faith through the lens of Scripture and has simply and movingly described what he sees: grace living and active in every aspect of our 'ordinary' experience. He not only contemplates God's presence in human life, but shows us how to do it for ourselves."

Bernard J. Bush, S.J.
Grace Institute

"Bill Huebsch points out that 'we do not learn grace so much as we are informed in it.' This book goes a long way in helping people understand how God is already moving in their lives. It restores a genuine concreteness to the meaning of grace."

Robert J. Schreiter
Co-editor, *New Theology Review*

"Through scriptural images and common experiences, this 'new look at grace' challenges us to see it as the most important aspect of our faith lives. The distinctive images and storytelling create an unforgettable journey to the mystery and wonder of the grace-filled reality of everyday experience."

Spiritual Book News

"The greatest need in the contemporary church is for people to learn how to recognize the action of God in their everyday lives. In stories, images, and examples, Bill Huebsch pushes, prods, and plays with the events and behavior of everyday life until they become transparent conveyors of grace. This is a wonderful refresher course for those who need to sharpen their vision of the Spirit at work in the ordinary."

Carolyn Osiek, RSCJ, Professor of New Testament
Catholic Theological Union of Chicago

"Here is a realistic book on grace that has both memory and vision. Bill Huebsch remembers what Catholics learned and how they lived years ago when everything seemed clear. He also knows how muddled things have become. More important, he has a clear vision of how things could be in the future. From his pen, grace once again is a gracious word, sensitive and mysterious. His book is wonderful."

Eugene LaVerdiere, sss
Editor, *Emmanuel*

CONTENTS

INTRODUCTION

In the spring of 1981, I was a graduate student at Catholic Theological Union in Chicago's Hyde Park. I had found at CTU a community of students and teachers devoted to exploring the great questions of truth which people everywhere have explored for centuries.

Early in my time at CTU, I fell under the influence of Rev. Gene LaVerdière and I began to probe the Scriptures deeply. The question that I brought to my work with Scripture is the very one that I am undertaking here. As I heard Gene LaVerdière work with the text, I knew that I had found my teacher.

There were other courses and other teachers as well who patiently stood by as I rediscovered much that had gone before me in coming to understand how it is that Jesus brings people to wholeness, to grace.

But in the spring of 1981, I was enrolled in a seminar studying Karl Rahner's theology. The professor's name was Peter Schineller, a Jesuit.

I could never forget what we did there that spring. Only about 15 of us had enrolled in the seminar and we spent the entire time together reading one book: Rahner's *Foundations*. We read and struggled with this text, guided by Peter and every secondary source that we could find.

As the semester slowly progressed, the excitement of the class began to grow because we were discovering grace!

It was as though the veil lifted slowly and we began to see clearly what that theology had been which stood behind the work done at Vatican II. We began to uncover what that understanding of grace had been which empowered the liturgical reformers, the formation movements of women religious, and the landmark work of the Scripture scholars earlier in this century.

Here it was: grace.

We realized that the hard work we were doing, to pore over Rahner paragraph by paragraph, would yield rich results. But it was very hard work and that course overshadowed everything else I did that term in school. What Rahner had to say was wonderful; coming to understand it was not.

"God himself," Rahner wrote for example in *Foundations* (p. 137), "as the abiding and holy mystery, as the incomprehensible ground of man's [sic] transcendent existence is not only the God of infinite distance, but also wants to be the God of absolute closeness in a true self-communication, and he is present in this way in the spiritual depths of our existence as well as in the concreteness of our corporeal history."

This is exciting stuff. But what does it mean?

That's the present question; the central purpose of this book is to lay it out in plain English. Theology must be common; it cannot remain hidden in heavy-duty theological jargon. I remember thinking during that seminar that if everyone who has left the church could read and understand this, and if everyone who has remained would interiorize it, the scales would fall from our eyes and we would see the energy of the resurrection of Christ standing tall before us, empowering not only the church, but the world.

There is a great danger in what I am doing here. This presentation of grace is almost entirely without nuance and there is the danger that, because of that, it may be misunderstood. But I think we must take this risk. In a sense, as a valuable theological reflection, this is a "discussion draft." I hope that you will argue with me—and with others—about this. Have I sometimes gone too far to be inclusive? Have I sometimes not gone far enough? Is it too harsh in places? too psychologized? too simple? or still too complex?

If what we understand about God in our lives and our world is not debated among all the people, then we risk losing the value of human experience which is where, Rahner helps us to see, God can most readily be found.

The opening line of the first chapter of this book summarizes my intent here, "There are some things about grace that everyone should know."

THE TITLE

There have been many trends in psychology since Freud first made his observations in the late nineteenth century. Most of these trends are reported in books that have lined the shelves of shopping mall bookstores since the early 1970s. For the most part, I do not trust those trends but they are useful inasmuch as they are part of the whole discussion which is slowly uncovering the human mind.

However, I suspect that at least one of those popular movements is not a trend but a lasting dimension of all human healing: the wholeness movement. The healing of the whole person: mind, body, spirit, and soul, is as old as the Hebrew and Christian Scriptures and common to religious understanding from East to West.

These reflections rise out of that rich history of healing and are a spirituality of wholeness. They seek to provide a basis for our belief that God wants us to be whole and that God's grace can empower us for that.

THE FORMAT

I've chosen not to present this material in common paragraph form. I hope this will not be confusing. There is an ancient writing style which presents prose in a format like this, allowing the reader freedom to pick up the development of ideas with the poetic side of the mind as well as the more logical side.

This method of presentation throws into greater relief the coordination and subordination of ideas. It presents certain parallel thoughts and even isolates key words and phrases in a way that the common paragraph style would not.

In this way, the text will yield to meditation more easily. It is meant to be read with frequent pauses. Put the book down in your lap from time to time as you read, and let the energy of the words well up around you.

1

WHY ARE WE
TALKING ABOUT GRACE?

There are some things that everybody should know
   about grace.

Most of us learned about grace
         when we were children
         in catechism class with Father
         or in grade school with Sister
         or somewhere from someone who "knew."
In those "good old days"
      we used to be able to
      be sure about grace
         and God
         and sin
         and all those things which
               we knew
               we either had to seek
               or to avoid
         in order to gain either heaven or hell.
But we're really not sure
      about anything religious any more,
      and we've sort of forgotten about
      this matter called grace.

      Most of us have,

from time to time,
memorized answers to questions
that dealt with all the great mysteries
of the church,
answers that laid them out
in a nice orderly fashion,
like pairs of shoes in a closet.
We really knew what was what!

The attempt was to get it all straight,
get it all down
and make sure that we understood
because then we'd be better Christians.
And also because then we could be assured
of "making it" in the Spiritual World.

So grace was one of those things
that we learned to know.
But the thing about grace was that,
even in those times of spiritual certainty,
we were never quite sure,
not quite absolutely sure
when we had it.
But we were damn sure when we didn't!
The rules about losing grace
seemed much clearer
than the ways of obtaining grace.

One of the very important questions
that all of us had on our minds
during those years
was:
"Am I in the state of grace?"
This was important
because if we weren't in the state of grace,
and we suddenly died,
we knew we would go straight to hell.
This was never a joking matter.

But we also knew
that we could,
    if we had the time,
    make a perfect act of contrition
    which would temporarily restore us to
        the state of grace,
        but only until we could make
        a good confession.

This was really a rather public matter for us
    because when everyone else
    got up to go to communion
    during Mass,
    everyone in the church knew
    who was not in the state of grace,
    because they couldn't go.
        They had to sit there
        marked as the dirty sinners they were
        while all the lines filed past
        on their way to the communion rail.
I used to wonder if people could guess
    why I didn't go to communion sometimes:
    "Do they know that I allowed an impure
    thought
        to linger longer than I should have?"

Certain terrible sins,
    you must remember,
    could remove all grace
        from our souls.
Certain actions or desires,
    even certain thoughts,
    could render us unfit for the Kingdom of God,
    and unpleasing enough to God so that
we would be sealed in our perdition for eternity.

But God, we were assured,
    would only send us to hell
    if we insisted on it.

There wasn't much discrimination here:
    priests, nuns, bishops, lay people—

all were fated alike
when it came to "losing grace."
And the sin that did it
could be anything from
tasting meat on a Friday
if you were Catholic
to murder
because both were "mortal sins."
It could be anything from that "impure" thought
allowed to linger for a moment
to adultery and fornication.

It was really very clear
if you knew the system.
The lines were quite distinct:
we knew what was a sin and what wasn't.
Nope, there was no doubt about it.

Now,
if you were ever in doubt
about what it took to
lose grace,
there was always someone nearby to ask:
your pastor.

Father pretty much always knew
and if he was out,
you could always ask the assistant pastor.
In any case,
someone official would always know
the answers.
The point here is that
in those days
there were answers in the first place.
We knew what was what
and we knew that the "official" church
would tell us.

And from certain sins
the pastor could even give a dispensation.
You could actually get permission in advance

to go ahead and "commit the sin"
but the punishment,
the loss of grace,
the threat of eternal damnation
would be removed
by the nod of the pastor's head.

It was a marvelous system
for controlling the flow of grace.

But it didn't stop here.
It was also possible
to store up grace
and to earn it for others.

Storing up grace was always said to be a good idea.
That way,
if you died unexpectedly
or if you accidentally committed a sin
without really realizing it
or if you just came up "short" on grace
for some reason,
you would have a little in your "account."
You could earn grace,
sort of like earning your allowance,
by doing good works,
by saying your prayers,
by using certain blessed objects,
by receiving certain blessings,
by giving good example,
by certain kinds of financial gifts,
and in a whole variety of other ways
but apparently not
just by asking for it.

Earning grace and storing it up was the business
of the spiritual life.
It was the preoccupation of those
seeking to be close to God.
It was the primary focus of effort
and the only way to heaven.

The trouble was
that it took only one
of those nasty mortal sins
to undo all your earnings.

One slip and your bank account was closed.
If you spent your whole life
   trying to be good
   but ate a hamburger for lunch on a Friday
   and died before you got to confession
      you went straight to hell.
(I don't think the church ever
   actually taught this on an official level
   but all the church's agents
      taught it fervently
      and believed it religiously.)

Earning grace for others was simpler
   and it was usually done
   after they'd died.
   It was a way to "earn" their way
   out of purgatory and into heaven.

So, as a general sort of review,
   that's the way it was,
   and, to some extent,
   that's the way it still is for many of us.
      But I hear people asking,
      from time to time:
         "What ever happened to sin?"
         "Didn't this used to be wrong?"
         "Is it OK to break the rules?"

Few of us adults have been to catechism class
   for a while.
   Most of us have had to depend
      on what we learned then
      even though
         it no longer serves us very well.
   For most of us,
      what we know
      about what the church teaches today
      has probably come from *Time* magazine.
   Most adult Christians
      learn more about their church
      from the popular press

than they do from
the pulpit
or any sort of religious event.

Many of us have forgotten
most of what we learned
when we were kids
because, for the most part,
the church has stopped talking
about those things in that way.

Many of us have committed certain serious sins
which we have failed to confess
and we have gone on in our lives
and hope to continue going on.
But the sins are there,
on our souls or somewhere,
and we aren't really sure
what to do about that.
We aren't even sure they were sins to begin with,
but the doubts linger for us,
they nag us,
they beg for attention,
they search for answers.
If we go to the "official" church for direction,
the leaders feel compelled
to answer the way they always have:
giving official answers
to our rather unofficial questions.
We get the sense,
in listening to these official answers,
that not even the pastor
believes this any longer.
Then we aren't sure what to believe,
except that we're sure
that we want to believe in something.

Many of us have learned to ignore
some of those childhood lessons in "religion"
and to live
with as much heart and goodness
as we can muster.
Many of us are tormented.
Some of us are afraid of God.

Some of us still count sins
as we do our shoes.
Some of us are in doubt.
Some of us don't know what to think any more,
and many of us have simply left the church
because it was easier to do that
than to unravel all those complicated
sins and indulgences.

Many people prefer to take the risk
that God will be merciful in the end
rather than struggle with a system
that no longer seems to meet their needs.

There is confusion in the church today
about all of this.
The confusion would be tolerable
except that many people's lives
are being lived in the shadow
of an historical albatross
over which they had no control
but which now threatens to control them.

So we need to look at all of this again.
We need to re-examine grace
and re-ask those questions we once memorized.
We need to talk together again
because,
while the truth about grace
has not changed,
the language we use to describe
that truth
has changed a great deal.

The language we learned as children,
the language our parents learned
and dozens of generations before them,
was a language of the twelfth century
later frozen in time
by anxious bishops
at the Council of Trent,
bishops fearful that without certainty,
all the known world would unravel.

But today,
    because of fearless people
    during the Council of Vatican II,
    we have a fresh language,
        a language of life and vitality,
        a language that promises
        to help those who take it seriously
        to move into the Heart of the Lord
            and the Heart of the Gospel.
The trouble with today's new expression
    of these ancient truths
    is that it is written in heavy-duty
    theological language,
        a language that I'm convinced
        not even all the theologians
            always understand.
We need to learn to talk
    about these things
    in plain, simple, everyday words,
        words that we understand.
    We take a risk in doing this
        that we will miss some of the nuances,
        some of the fine points,
        some of the minor distinctions,
        of the greater theological argument.
That would be a problem,
    if it was the theological argument
    that we were concerned with
    in the first place.
But it isn't and we aren't.

We are concerned with getting on
    with our spiritual lives
    and finding some guidance in the
    fresh and exciting
    ways of talking about these things
        that we have available today.

So we need to talk about grace again
    because there are some things about grace
    that everybody should know.

2

LIFE IS MYSTERIOUS

Grace is perhaps the most important
   aspect of our faith.

Part of the evidence
      is that it has been
            the theology of grace
            over which church leaders have disagreed
            for centuries:

Is the grace of God sufficient that we are
      saved by faith alone?
Or is grace such that,
      in order to obtain it,
      we must also perform good works
      in order to be saved?

Does grace have the power to change us
      interiorly, permanently, or essentially?
Or does it merely cover over our sinful natures
      which remain sinful,
      despite the presence of grace?

Is grace something given freely by God to all?
Or is it meted only to those who fulfill
            certain prescriptions
            of the law?

Is it really possible for a person
  to lose grace completely?
Can a human being who has lost grace
  go on living?
  Or does that person die?

Grace seems so important
  and yet we know so little.
Most people,
  if asked,
  which they rarely would be,
  wouldn't know what to say
  if someone wanted them to define grace.
Most people,
  if they thought about it much,
  which they rarely do,
  would appear not to be affected
  on a day-to-day basis
  by grace,
    whatever it is.
Most people,
  if push came to shove,
  which it really does quite often,
  would take their chances with the mercy of God
  rather than relying on theology
  which doesn't always
  succeed in guiding people
  to recognize grace.
Most people,
  if it stood right before them,
  which it does every day,
  wouldn't have the faintest idea
  what grace even is
  or what it means to experience it
  or even what it all has to do with God
    or Christ
    or sin
    or heaven
    or hell
      or any of that stuff.

Grace is like that.

It eludes our grasp
    and our understanding
    and our academic probing and pursuit.
It is radically present in our lives,
    yet it cannot be touched
    or even seen.
And the minute we try
    to capture grace,
    to corner the market on it,
        it seems to disappear into thin air.
No explanation is sufficient.

In this way,
    grace is just like being human.
Who could adequately define what that means?

Oh,
we could give a scientific explanation,
    defining the cells and impulses of the body,
    or we could even
    make a beginning in understanding the brain.
But who can define the Mind?
    Who can explain the Human Spirit?
    Who could describe Personality?
    Who can touch the Soul?

Human beings,
    us:
    we stand constantly
        at the very edge of mystery.
Much of what makes us tick is mysterious;
    so mysterious that,
    even after all these years
    of medical probing,
    we still do not very well understand
    our mind and soul.
Our whole lives open into
    a kind of endlessness,
    a horizon reaching beyond our sight.

We are always reaching
　another threshold on that horizon,
　yet we never reach
　the end of human potential.
　　We jump farther,
　　run faster,
　　discover more,
　　probe farther into space,
　　and every year find yet another horizon.

It is as though
　we stand
　on the edge of a great primeval forest
　looking out across
　a great, unexplored, sunlit savannah:
　　Dare we venture out
　　　into that unknown?
Dare we not?

But as we stand on the edge of that mystery
　the edge of that endless horizon
　of discovery,
　of energy,
　of love and laughter,
we do not stand there alone.
Deep within our spirit,
　buried in our bones,
　kept as a secret in our hearts,
　stirring our bowels,
　　is a greater mystery yet,
　　an energetic mystery
　　that both draws us toward it
and is the source of our power to proceed.
We don't know much about this
　other mysterious force
　except that it seems sure to be there.

We have all experienced this:
　we come along in our lives
　day in and day out,

until we come to something that
we simply cannot explain:
   death
   illness
   beauty
   love
   birth
   friendship
   well-being
   or whatever.
At those times, we find ourselves
   moving forward,
   empowered by an energy
   that we do not understand and moving toward
      a new personal space
      a new freedom
      a new self-knowledge
      a new strength
      a new and greater depth.
We say that we do not know
   where we ever got the strength
   and that is correct:
This source of strength
   and this new growth
      both exceed our grasp.

If we are reflective
   we know it is present
   but we really do not know
   much else about it.
It is ultimately beyond our comprehension.

But we take a certain comfort in knowing
   that this mysterious force
   is there.
So we call on this mysterious energy
   for healing
   peace
   and love,
and we name it: God.

"God," we should remember,
    is our name for it,
    not its name for itself.

This experience of mystery
    is something that everyone has:
        it is not limited to Christians
        and certainly not to Catholics.
It can form a deep bond of human solidarity;
    draw us together into one;
    bind us tightly to one another.

There is not very much
    that we can say with certainty
    about this Holy Mystery.
But despite that, we have
    been talking about it
    through the ages.
We have even fought wars about it,
    of all things!

In the end,
we have only our human experience
    of mystery to go on.
That may not seem like much,
    but when
    we collect our experiences together:
    write them down,
    tell stories about them,
    celebrate them,
    and reflect about them,
we find that there is more
    there than we thought.
But even when we probe this
    and study it
    and establish schools of theology
        to explore it deeply,
we find that the mystery
    eludes us.

After all of this,
    we find that our best bet
    is simply to loosen our grip,
    lighten up,
and let mystery be Mystery.

When we stand back a bit
    and let that happen,
    we find this Mystery
        gently revealing us to ourselves.

Let's get concrete about this:
    How does this really happen
    in our everyday lives?
That's the real question.

Our experiences of everyday living vary quite a lot,
    but choose one of these,
    or make up one of your own,
    and we will trace the movement into mystery
    that we have been describing here:
        someone dies
        you wake up feeling sick
        the sunrise is gorgeous
        you realize that you're gay
        your child is in trouble
        you've just heard a moving poem
        you feel a little restless today
        the doctor says you have cancer
        you give an anonymous gift to someone
        you have an overwhelming sense
            of well-being
        you kiss and make up with someone
        an old friend calls just to visit
        a song brings back old memories
        you commit that same old sin again.
These are common, everyday,
    ordinary human experiences.
But they hold the potential for
    divine revelation.
How do these experiences lead us to Holy Mystery?

First,
    they will not do so,
    absolutely cannot do so,
    unless we pause in our day to reflect on them.
Pausing is without question the first step.

I'm convinced that those who first formed
    the prayer of the church
    knew this in their bones.
They established
    a series of regular times for prayer
    in every day.
These times,
    it was hoped,
    would lead people to reflection
    on the mysteries
    on a regular, periodic basis,
        day in and day out.
Unfortunately,
    two things went wrong with that prayer form.
One was that
    it became so methodical
    that no one paid much attention to it.
        People started "saying" their prayers,
        rather than really praying.
    That's really too bad.
Prayer is natural to humans,
    it is our natural orientation to pray.
We do it all the time,
    naturally. It's how we're made:
    We are oriented to Mystery.
The other was that
    it got into somebody's head one time
    that the only valid mysteries
    on which to reflect
    were purely "divine" mysteries.
I'm not sure how this started
    but it takes us down the wrong track.

The divine, holy Mystery
is absolutely unfathomable
incomprehensible
inexhaustible
essentially unsolvable
and wholly other.
All that we can know of this Mystery
comes to us through our
everyday human experiences.

Everything we say
about God
is really a statement about ourselves,
someone once observed.
But everything we say
about ourselves
is also a statement about God.

So pausing to reflect
on the mysterious stuff
of ordinary,
everyday life,
is what will lead us ultimately to
the Holy Mystery we seek.
Pausing in our day,
several times,
pausing to reflect
on the last couple of hours,
is the first step.
This Holy Pause
doesn't have to take a lot of time:
really two minutes will do it.
Pause and ask yourself this question:
What has gone on in this time
that holds the potential for Mystery?
At first,
it might not be easy or obvious,
but after you practice it for a while,
you'll be amazed at how quickly
you'll recognize Mystery.

What has gone on?
>Why did John call me?
>Where did that idea come from?
>What a gorgeous tree!
>Why does my friend love me like that?
>What makes me feel sick?
>Why am I so nervous?
>>and so forth.
Unless we pause,
>we will miss the potential for Mystery
>contained in these moments.
We will go rushing on,
>trying in vain to find meaning,
>trying to be satisfied,
>trying to find comfort and rest,
>>when all along,
>>the meaning,
>>the satisfaction of the heart,
>>and the rest we seek,
>>>is right there,
>>>waiting to be encountered.
The Holy Pause is very important.

Second,
>once we have paused to encounter Holy Mystery,
>we need to share it with someone else
>>and we need to do this often.
How often? Every day.

That seems like a lot of sharing
>to those of us
>who are out of the habit of sharing.
But, in fact,
>we will find,
>once we begin,
>that we will hunger for this daily bread,
>we will long for this opening,
>this putting-into-words
>>of the stuff of our lives.

Sharing like this,
  which is sometimes called "storytelling,"
  can take several forms:
    a phone call or a letter
    will do it,
  but the most immediate form,
  the most energizing form,
  the most clarifying form,
    is a simple, personal visit with someone.

I'm convinced that daily Mass
  began this way.
It was a time for people to gather,
  to share their lives.
A very appropriate
  context for this kind of sharing
  is a daily meal.
    Families
    communities
    friends:
we can all do this if we want to.

Sharing is important.
It takes the otherwise still somewhat abstract
  thoughts and observations
  of life,
  and puts words on them,
  makes them concrete,
  brings them out into reality,
  gives them air,
  lets them be challenged,
    clarified,
    and owned.

Here's the exciting part: we do this naturally.
It's a part of our nature
  to process our lives this way.
But often this processing
  becomes only chatter,
  it becomes a news report,
  a safe, almost antiseptic
  newsy little summary
that doesn't give way to meaning.

Because Holy Mystery
    both gives us to fear
    yet lures us toward itself,
    we tend to avoid the encounter.
To encounter Holy Mystery,
    however,
        is to encounter our very Selves.
So,
like the Holy Pause,
    this Holy Sharing,
    can lead us to ultimate meaning
    and can ultimately lead us
    to our full Selves.
We have to learn
    how to talk in this way.
    We are quite accustomed to non-talk,
    to chatter,
    and we have to re-learn
    how to share.

So first the Holy Pause and then the Holy Sharing:
    What's next?

All of this is rooted
    beyond the ordinary storytelling
    of daily life
in the Great Stories of our Holy Writings.

Here,
in the gospels and letters of the Scriptures,
    we find the Jesus story,
    which is what nourishes and sustains
    and gives meaning
    to our own everyday stuff.
We need to find a way,
        on a daily basis,
        to hear this Word.

But I don't think this means
    that we have to speed through the text.

Rather,
    taking one story at a time,
    maybe for a week or more,
    and letting it sink into our marrow
    will provide a deeper meaning.
But we need to do more than read it.
    We also need to study it.
Scripture scholarship is readily available today.
There is no excuse for any of us
    not looking beyond the Bible for more.
By looking further,
    we will discover the historical
    editorial
    literary
    faith-filled context
        in which it was written.
These are,
    after all,
    the stories of the Community.
That's great stuff.

They take us beyond ourselves,
    beyond our everydayness,
    into the great common stories
    which shed light,
    or, in other words,
        which enlighten
            our own stories every day.
Without the stories of Scripture
    we will never make meaning of our own stories.

But here's the key:
    we need to read it and be familiar with it,
    we need to study it and learn its meaning,
    but eventually
    we also need to share it with someone else.

Just as we do with the stories
from our lives,
we need also to share this story.

This isn't easy:
we are in such a habit of being private
about "religion."

We need to learn to speak
to one another.
For example, we might say
to a friend:
"This has been going on in my life,
or that has,
and these are my feelings and fears.
But I've been mindful
of this or that particular story
from the Gospel,
and this is what I think all of this
might mean for me...."

We will find a rhythm in this:
a couple Sacred Pauses in our day,
a time of Sacred Sharing with another,
a time with the Sacred Stories of Scripture
and finally, gathering now and then,
with friends and neighbors and family,
to celebrate all of this
with singing and dancing,
storytelling,
laughing and crying,
liturgizing,
eating and drinking.
We gather ourselves together,
the ins and outs of life,
the ups and downs.
And we bring along the memories,
the dreams,
and the stories.

We bring it all together in one place
    with the elements of earth:
        bread and water and wine,
    and we summarize life,
    we celebrate it.

Then this Great and Holy Mystery
    which we encounter along our way,
    yields profound meaning
    and we realize that
        without it now,
        without that encounter each day,
            we could not go on living.

Now, you see,
    the ordinary stuff of everyday living
    has become the stuff
of which divine revelation is made.

We learn who we really are
    by reflecting on how we really live
    and by holding that up
        against the stories of Scripture.
When we are revealed to ourselves
    in divine revelation that way,
    those moments of
    discovery
are really moments of grace.

Grace, then,
    is when God communicates God-self to us
    by revealing us to ourselves
    in the context of community sharing
    about everyday events in our lives
    and the words of Holy Scripture.

3

GRACE LEADS TO DENIAL

Do you remember the story
about Peter in the courtyard
during the trial of Jesus?
It's a haunting story
if you read it
from the point of view of grace.

It's usually thought
by preachers
by teachers
and by others in the know
that in the story
Peter denied Jesus.
In fact,
the story itself is often called
by that title,
"Peter's denial of Jesus."

But I have never been convinced
that that is what happened there,
at least not directly.

The Gospel from John's community
tells this story of denial most poignantly.
In this version of the story,
there is a small crowd of folks

gathered around a charcoal fire
near where the trial of Jesus is taking place.
The juxtaposition with the trial
    is obviously no accident:
    Peter is on trial, too.

(The charcoal fire is also important,
but more about that later.)

Now you must remember
    that all of the other disciples
    had run off,
        frightened.
The text tells us that only Peter
    followed Jesus,
    and even then at quite a distance.
It would be most fair to conclude
    that Peter was afraid as he stood
    by that charcoal fire.
He was afraid, but at least he was there.

So one of the other people there
    comes up to Peter and tells him the truth:
    "You are one of them, aren't you?"
    meaning,
        "You are the person
        who lives in company with Jesus."

Remember that this is the gospel
    in which we have heard Jesus teach us:
    "You will know the truth
    and the truth will make you free."
But clearly in this case
    the truth was not making Peter very free
    and he denied that he knew Jesus.

But notice, please,
    he did not deny that Jesus was Jesus,
    he did not deny that Jesus had been
    all he'd said he would be.

He did not deny Jesus,
    he denied himself:
        "I am not," he said,
        "I am not one of them."
He didn't do it just once or twice,
    he denied himself three times.
Obviously,
    he meant what he said.

This threefold self-denial
    carries a deep, profound meaning
    to the hearer of the word.
It might be possible for someone to
    commit a certain offense once
    and later repent,
    learning to live with imperfection.
Who hasn't done this?
    Who among us hasn't gone ahead
        and lied
        or stole
        or masturbated
        or gossiped
        or been lazy
        or selfish
        or cruel,
    only later to recognize the evil
    and repent,
    promising never to do it again?

But it is more difficult to see the evil
    if the offenses become habits.
We learn to become hardened to the guilt,
    in this case a healthy guilt,
    and we ignore the warning signs
    that come through our interior lives,
    the signs that warn us
    to stop and turn around now
    before it is too late
    and we become the victims
        of darkness.

So the second self-denial
    was clearly a sign that Peter
    was becoming locked in himself
        and locked out of the life of Jesus.

But,
the third time!
    Oh, that third time,
    that is the ultimate time:
    for now Peter was stepping into
        a dangerous
        dark
        and self-determined hell.
The third time, Peter was playing with fire!

(We'll come back to that charcoal fire in a
minute.)

When I hear this story,
    I can hear echoing behind it
    the denial of self
    that good people throughout the ages
    have fallen into the habit of practicing.
Good people, these,
    who cannot or will not admit the truth
    about themselves
    and who,
    in the denial of themselves,
        even though they be "churched" people,
deny Jesus.

Deny Jesus?

Yes.
That is exactly what we do
    when we deny who we are.
Jesus told us:
    "I am the truth."

That is a powerful self-description.
"I am the truth."
I am the truth about
who you are...
what you need...
who you love...
what you've done...
I am the truth about you.

So to deny the truth
is to deny Jesus.
Having faith in Jesus
means having faith in the truth
means having faith in myself.

I can hear the alcoholic saying
"I'm no drunk!"
"I'm not an alcoholic."
"I am not one of these."
(Three times: can you hear the rooster crow?)

I can hear the wealthy people saying
"I've earned it!"
"But it's all mine."
"I am not one of these."

I can hear the self-righteous saying
"But she had an abortion!"
"But he's not in fashion!"
"But they're living together in sin!"
"I am not one of these."

I can hear the homosexual saying
"I deny it!"
"It's not true."
"I am not one of these."

I can hear the lonely person saying
"I'm OK."
"Don't bother with me."
"I am not one of these."

I can hear the stubborn people saying
   "I don't have to accept new things."
   "I don't need to grow."
   "I am not one of these."

Good people all of these,
   but people in the habit
   of denying their very selves.

The list goes on: the military bomber
   the male elite
   the nuclear bomb builder
   the thief
   the liar
   the abortionist
   the violent
   the anti-Semite
   the selfish
   the grudge-holder
   the gossip
   the abuser
   the apathetic
   the faithless
and on and on and on....

Again and again we hear the truth:
   "Surely you are one of these."
And again and again we deny it steadfastly:
   "I am not," we say,
      "I am not one of these."

But the truth is that we are. We all are.
There is no denying it.

Now picture this for a moment:
   It's a damp, cold night.
      Why else would you need a charcoal fire?
   You are standing with a bunch of strangers
      in a dark alley-like place.

Your best friend is on trial
    for insisting on doing things
    that you yourself had tried to
    talk him or her out of.
From nowhere come these strangers
accusing you of being part of your friend's
    crazy carryings-on.
Not just once or twice,
    but three times
    they accuse you of it.
You are frightened,
    confused
    frustrated
    cold
        and alone.
You can't face the fact
    that this is who you've become.
You hadn't noticed
    that slowly, over the years,
    this is who you'd really become.
        You have become one of these.
You are in the habit of denying
    this in yourself
    because maybe you really don't want
        this to be true.
So when you are confronted like this,
    you deny that this is who you are.

But in your heart,
    you know the truth.

Let's go back to that charcoal fire for a minute.
In the story as John tells it,
    Jesus is convicted
    killed
    buried
and that's that.

The disciples try to get on with their lives.
They try,
    but they are restless.
They go from one thing to another,
    not really able to get into anything.
    They try this and that to stay busy:
        they are trying to forget.

But forgetting someone as dramatic in their lives
    as Jesus had been
    will not be easy.
He was,
    after all,
the truth of their very lives.
He lived within them,
    as well as alongside them.
Now the comfort of his
    physical presence is gone,
    but not the truths
    that he'd revealed to them.
He haunts them:
    his words
    his actions
    his love for them
    his friendship
    his care
    his truth-telling.
They just can't forget.
They've done the crying.
They've talked about him endlessly for days,
    maybe even for weeks.
Then one night
    they are sitting down by the sea,
    the sea that they remember Jesus loved.
There are seven of them there:
    Peter, of course,
    Thomas, who doubted
    Nathanael, the one from Cana
    James and John, the sons of Zebedee
    and two others but we can't
        remember who they were.

There were seven:
    it's as though the whole church was there.

It was clearly another one of those nights:
    they were restless,
    unable to forget,
    sulking around,
    not satisfied,
    not at ease,
        not peaceful.
One of them would get up.
    He'd toss a stone into the lake.
    Then another would wonder aloud
        where he'd go from here.
Then a third would wish again
    that he hadn't run off, leaving Jesus behind.

Finally Peter, impulsive Peter, had had it.
    "I can't take it any more!" he said,
    "I'm getting out of here: let's go fishing."
So off they went.

Can't you just see the seven of them:
    there in the dark,
    crowded into a boat designed for three,
    fishing in the night?

But,
that's what they'd been doing with
    their lives:
fishing in the dark.
That's what happens when people
    begin denying themselves:
    they live in darkness.
Then the text of John's Gospel says,
    as the light began to break
    someone was standing on the beach.
The writer is careful to let us know who it is,
    but careful to note as well
    that the fishing party in the story
    was still in the dark about it:
        they did not know it was Jesus.

So this guy on the beach says,
    "Hey! Have you folks caught any fish?"
"No," they told him.
    "This must be a lousy place to fish."
    These guys had been trying their best
        to figure all this out.
    They'd been trying to own up to
        who they really were.
    They'd been working hard
        at working out their lives.
And then,
    when they just couldn't do it any more,
    they gave up:
"I'm just a lousy person, that's all."

Peter's denial of himself there
    in front of that charcoal fire
    was a denial that all the followers of Jesus
    had gone through.
All of us had been on trial with Jesus.
All of us were being judged:
    "Are you the person you were created to be?"
    "Or have you become someone else?"
    "Isn't this really who you are?"
And all of us,
    all of us,
    along with Peter,
    have denied our very
        selves.
It is for all of us
    a time of great darkness,
    a dark night of truth.

So here's this guy on the beach
    telling them now to keep going:
"Throw your nets on the other side of the boat!"

Why hadn't they thought of that?
I wonder.
I mean,
these fishers were professionals;
they used to do this for a living.
Could they possibly have been fishing all night
without trying the right side of the boat?
But they tried it anyway, one more time,
and lo!
their nets were filled:
one hundred and fifty-three large fish!
And that's a lot of fish.

When this happened,
John, one of Jesus' closest friends,
finally realizes that the guy on the beach
is Jesus.
The lights come on all around
and everyone can see it now.

Haven't we done that?
Haven't we recognized Jesus like that?

The text is clear:
as the dawn is breaking over our lives,
as the light begins to scatter the darkness,
as we begin to find our way
and make our catch,
it will dawn on us:
the one calling to us,
the one giving the directions,
the one standing there unnoticed
until now
is Jesus.
When we finally see that,
then we are enlightened.
And then,
for the first time in our lives,
we begin to
experience resurrection.

Then the story goes on to say that Peter,
    impulsive Peter,
    naked Peter,
    when he realized that it was Jesus,
    put on his garments and jumped into the water.
We've all done that:
    we've caught a glimpse of Jesus on the shore,
    or our parents did,
    and we put on the garment of baptism
    and jumped into the waters of new life.

The story goes on to tell us
    that the very next thing they did together
    was to share a meal,
a breakfast fish fry on the beach.

This is probably the first real meal these
disciples
    have had in days:
    you know how hard it is to eat
    when you feel restless.
In fact,
    it's probably their
    first real meal
    since that last supper
        they'd had with Jesus.

And the meal took place over a charcoal fire.
It was a meal, no doubt,
    of thanksgiving: a eucharist.
    What were they thankful for?
        Undoubtedly, they were grateful
        for each other:
        for being embraced by this warm,
            human community of faith.

And it was over that charcoal fire
    the same fire over which Peter had run away
    from himself,
        and thereby
        run away from Jesus,
    over this same fire now,
        that Peter would come home.

But this isn't the damp, dark night of the trial,
    alone with strangers,
    accusing Peter of the truth.
No,
    this is a quiet morning,
    a gentle lake lapping at the shore,
    friends,
    light,
    a good meal,
    comfort in being with Jesus.
And Jesus confronts Peter with the truth,
    the same truth he had denied earlier,
    the truth which is Jesus.
But this time it is different.
This time it is a confrontation in love:
    "Peter, do you love me?"
    "Peter, are you one of mine?"
    "Peter, are you one of these?"

"Yes, my friend," Peter responds, "yes, I am.
    I am one of these!"
And Peter had come home to himself.

4

GRACE IS ENERGIZING

In the story about Peter's denial
   of himself
   and, thereby, of Jesus,
   we learn a great deal about
      grace and empowerment.
The two go hand-in-hand:
   when Peter finally seized
   the personal power
   to be his ownmost self,
      then he was also stimultaneously seized
      by the grace of Jesus.

At the same time,
   it was the grace of Jesus
   that enabled him
   to be his ownmost self
in the first place.

All of the gospels are filled with talk
   about empowerment.

From the announcements of the angels,
   first to Mary
   and then to the shepherds,
to the commissioning of the apostles
   after the resurrection,

the gospels repeatedly
    refer to the empowerment of God.

Do you remember the time
    Jesus was in the synagogue?
    He had gone there
    after coming out of the desert.
The text is clear about this:
    "Jesus returned
        in the power of the Spirit,"
        the text says,
        and then it goes on to tell this story:
Jesus went to Nazareth,
    which was where he'd lived as a child.
His adult home was probably in Capernaum
    so this was like a homecoming for him.

He went to the synagogue,
    which he was in the habit of doing
    on the sabbath day.
He stood up to read
    (probably because he was a guest there)
    and he was given a copy of the Scriptures,
    in particular
    the book of the prophet Isaiah.
The text gives a lot of detail here:
    he opened the book
    he found the place he wanted
    he began to read
    he read
    he closed the book
    he gave it back to the attendant
    he sat down:
a very dramatic storytelling.

But what he read was even more dramatic:
    "The Spirit of the Lord is upon me,"
        it began,

"...he has anointed me,
    empowered me,
        to preach
        to proclaim release
        to give sight
        to set free
    and to proclaim the year of the Lord."
It was no wonder that
    the eyes of all were fixed upon him
    after he sat down.
This had been a demonstration
    of tremendous power.

There were many other times
    in the gospels
    where this power was demonstrated.
For example,
    one day
    Jesus had gathered some folks around him;
        they were attracted to him
        and to his teachings.
On this particular occasion,
    he taught a large group for a long time
    on the side of a mountain near his home.
We have come to call that occasion
    "The Sermon on the Mount."
After he was finished with his work that day,
    the text tells us
    that the people wondered aloud
    how he could speak with such power
        with such authority.
In fact, the text says that the people
    who had heard him that day
    were absolutely astonished at his power!

That happens sometimes
    when there is a great speaker:
    the crowd becomes enthused
    energized
    filled with power.

Only in this case,
    it was more than that:
It was more than merely seeing someone powerful:
    this crowd was empowered by Jesus.

That is,
        the power of God,
        so present in Jesus of Nazareth that day,
        was not used as a means
        of over-powering others
            but rather of em-powering them.
That's why the crowds were so astonished.
        They simply weren't accustomed to having
        people in authority
        do anything but over-power them.

Michael Crosby has helped us to see that
        this way that God has of sharing with us,
        of em-powering us through Christ,
        this is Grace!

And what does this Grace empower us to do?
It is the Grace to be our ownmost selves,
        to be the persons we are meant to be,
        to live out our created purpose,
        to come home to ourselves.
Just look at the Sermon on the Mount
        which precedes the astonishment of the crowds:

"Are you poor in Spirit?"
        Jesus would ask.
"Then you have God's favor
        God's power
        God's grace."

"Are you meek?
"Do you hunger for justice?
"Are you merciful to others?
"Are you a peacemaker?"
        Jesus would ask.
        "Then you are filled with God's love
        God's power
        God's grace."

"Be who you are," Jesus is saying.
    "Be the person you are created to be."
    "Be fully yourself."
    "Anybody who is created by God,
        which includes all of you,
        is created to be somebody.
    Don't become nobody,
        don't give away this power
            to be yourself,
        don't deny my grace to you.
Instead,
come home to yourselves."
It was quite a sermon, wasn't it?

When Jesus described
    what it is like to be in the kingdom of God,
    he used a powerful image:
    "The kingdom,"
    he said,
    "is within you."
"Don't go looking here and there;
    don't think you can find it outside of yourself.
No.
The kingdom you seek is within.
    And,
    when you find it,
    it will be like the person
    who finds a precious gem:
        you would trade nothing for it!"

How true that is!
We search and search for our identity
    and when we finally find ourselves,
    created
    rooted in Christ
    loved eternally,
then there is nothing that we would trade!

Later on one time,
Jesus had spent some apparently healing time
   with a young crippled man.
The time they spent together was such
   that Jesus could say to him
   in the context of their friendship,
     "Be of good cheer, my friend,
     your sins are forgiven!"
It must have been a great moment for both of them!
   A time of real intimacy,
   real sharing,
   real truth-telling,
and, finally, real healing.
But some of the religious hierarchy
   of that day
   were threatened and offended
   by this intimacy
   this healing
   this forgiveness
   this reconciliation
     and this power.
After all, the crippled guy
   hadn't even been to confession!
   and they would have presumed
   that he was crippled
   in the first place
     because of his sins.
So they challenged Jesus.
"No problem," Jesus told them.
   "This power I have is to be shared.
   Here, let me show you."
And with that,
   Jesus empowered this young man
   to come after him,
   to follow him,
   in a word, to take up his pallet and walk.

As he did this;
he said he was doing it
in order to demonstrate the
empowering, unconditional love
of God.
The text repeats for us,
in the very next line,
that the crowds were floored!
They had seen the power of God,
the Grace of God.

And in the very next breath of the text,
the very next verse,
Jesus calls Matthew
from his life of darkness
and gives him a new energy,
an energy to be his real self,
an energy to leave his un-real self behind:
the energy of grace.
Just imagine the relationship that this line
of the text is summarizing:
Jesus and Matthew must have spent
quite a little time together,
enough time, at least,
that Matthew, freed by the trust
the acceptance
the honesty
the gaze
of Jesus,
could be empowered to make new choices,
could be graced to become his real
full
created
Self.
What a great and powerful thing the love of God,
expressed in Christ,
can be for us!

The gospel goes on and on in describing
the empowerment of God!
In the very next chapter,
for example,
Jesus calls a group of his followers
to himself
and sends them out to preach and teach and heal.
But he doesn't just send them,
he empowers them!
The text is clear:
"He gave them authority...."
He empowered them.
He gave them Grace.

And at the end of the gospel story,
the writer gives the crowning moment
in the life of Christ
and in the purpose of Christ's life,
which was to empower the human family
to live up to its real self,
its created self.
Jesus is pictured with the ones who followed him
and he is preparing them for the work
of building the church.
In doing this, Jesus sends them to all the nations
invites them to baptize
asks them to teach
and promises to be with them.
But,
before he does all this,
the text tells us,
he empowers them!
He gives them the grace they will need.

We are very close now
to understanding that we are empowered
to be our ownmost selves
and that,
when we accept that empowerment
in faith,
then we accept Christ as well.

Then we become persons-for-others,
  persons sent to heal
  persons empowered for ministry
    in our everyday lives.

The very stuff of alienation
  of sin
  of suffering
  and of fear in us
    becomes the stuff
    that our ministry is made of.
"Our weakness becomes our strength."

Then we discover
  that in the moment of accepting
    grace and power
    we become powerless.
We discover
  that we become full
  only when we are empty.
We discover
  that we will live
  only when we willingly die.

And at this moment,
  this moment of powerlessness and emptiness
  something absolutely astonishing happens for us:
    We experience healing
    and we begin to become whole again.
    We experience reconciliation
      in our lives;
And we realize that
  we never really finish with this.

Concretely,
  this being empowered
  is a process of taking back responsibility
  for our own lives.
We take back who we really are.

We become our ownmost selves again,
and we find that our ownmost self
is always a self-for-others.
This taking-back
is done
not with hate or anger,
but with a profound love,
a love that in turn empowers others.

But who do we take it back from?
For some
it is necessary to regain self
from one's spouse.
Married people sometimes give each other
too much control over their lives.
For others
it is friends to whom they surrender
themselves.
For still others
it is old memories,
old sins,
the old days.
Some others give themselves
to religious groups of various kinds:
to cults
to ideologies such as
individualism
capitalism
racism
sectarianism
sexism
communism
or consumerism.
For many it is a favorite compulsion:
smoking
drinking
masturbating
stealing
lying
working

sleeping
praying
eating
or whatever.
For most people,
how they live is determined by
materialism and consumerism.
These people allow society to dictate their
behaviors and responses.
Fashion becomes their god.

Clearly,
in order to live in the grace of Jesus,
the power of God,
and the power of light,
we need to take back our life
from all these alienating forces around us.

We need to become our ownmost selves again.

Now,
I know what's going on inside of you:
You're thinking,
"That's easy for you to say!
Anybody can tell us this!
That's easier said than done!"
And you're right, of course.

But there is something else here,
something that helps
to make this circle complete:
We are not alone.
And Jesus was not alone either.

We often misunderstand this in the gospels.
We think,
Well, Jesus was God.
He was all-powerful.
He didn't have to deal with life the way I do.

This attitude
accounts for a lot of people
assuming that Jesus never had to
practice what he preached.
People assume that Jesus was God.

And, it's true:
Jesus is God. No doubt about it.
But he is also human,
very human
completely human
humanly human.
He ate
drank
slept
urinated
sweated
wept
worried
wondered
sang
told stories
was aroused
worked
got blisters
made mistakes
and generally was a regular type of guy.

Jesus was human and he faced all that humans face.
He wasn't half human and half divine,
Gene LaVerdière has pointed out,
you know,
sort of human on his mother's side
and divine on his father's side!
No.
He was fully human, fully divine.
This is mysterious and hard to understand,
but it is also very important.

Let's look at this from the point of view of grace.
Jesus was human,
    born of Mary,
    and he experienced the grace
    that all humans can:
    the grace of first breath,
    the grace of functioning lungs
    the grace of working bowels,
    in sum,
    the grace of the energy of life.
Grace is experienced
    in a physical way like that,
    we know this,
    and it's why we pray for physical healing
    when we are sick.

It's also why we even have a
    sacrament of healing
    in the church.

But there was more.
There is more for all of us.
    Jesus also experienced
    the immediate power
    of love
    of acceptance
    of being cared for by others.
What a wonderful power!
What a wonderful grace!
    And growing up in that home,
    with a woman full of grace,
        full of power,
        full of peace,
and with a man who was as good as they come,
    Jesus would experience
    many other forms of grace:
        the power of forgiveness,
        the power of kindness
        the power of hospitality
        the power of tears

the power of affection
the power of sex
the power of sharing
the power of work
the power of friendship
the power of honesty
the power of prayer
the power of reading Scripture
the power of poverty
the power of peace.

All of this grace,
   all working together,
   channeled through those others
   with whom he shared life,
this grace filled Jesus,
   filled him full of grace and power.

So it came as no surprise,
   I would imagine,
   to those who knew him well,
   that when he began to speak
      his words were full of power,
   and that when he began to heal,
      his acts were full of power as well.
I would think that anyone who knew him
   would not have been surprised at all
   that he would have been a peacemaker,
      a lover,
      a healer,
      a teacher,
      and, above all,
a friend to those he lived among.

This is the point:
Grace,
   which comes from God,
   and is God,

comes through the powerful acts of those around us,
    the acts of love,
    selflessness
    forgiveness
    and affection.
This grace,
    of which Jesus was full,
    this grace is the life of God.

The life of God is itself powerful
    creative
    and energizing
and Jesus was full of that!

God gave Godself to the world in this
    wonderful, yet almost frightening way.
    "God so loved the world," the text says,
    "that God sent that one
    which was most a part of Godself:
        Jesus."

Do you realize what this means?
    This means that God's own life,
    God's energy
    God's grace
        is within us.
And it means that we are empowered,
    (empowered!)
to energize others
    by loving them
    forgiving them
    accepting them
    and creating them.
This is no small potatoes kind of thing.
    The powerful ones we know
    are usually said to be
        the ones with money
        with importance
        with big jobs
        with lots of guns
            or whatever.

But we are talking here
    about a power far greater than that!
This is a power that can do marvelous things:
    it can heal
    bind together
    give comfort
    offer affection
    rest peacefully
    create new persons
    forgive
and if we would ever really accept
this power,
        the way that Jesus and Mary did:
            accept it completely
            and embrace it with our whole selves,
            then we could also forge
a new way for the human family to live together:
    then it would feed the hungry
    give drink to the thirsty
    visit the imprisoned
    clothe the naked
    and heal the sick.
No other power will do it. This is all we've got.

5

ON BEING NAKED

Something that has always been very striking to me
is that, even though it is true
that in the gospel story
Jesus died naked,
I rarely see a crucified image of him
without clothing.
Jim Lopresti has helped us understand that
this is a curious reinterpretation
of the gospel
on the part of
the ones in charge of making our images;
probably zealous people
who must think that it would be "impure"
to picture Jesus naked,
especially his genitals.

Like most of us,
these good people
are likely afraid of their own nakedness,
both emotional and physical,
and so believe that they must
deny Jesus his.

We have probably done this in order
to prevent "perverts"
from distorting the gospel
and desecrating Jesus
but in the very act of prevention,
we have ourselves
created a worse distortion than we have prevented.

I think the text easily
supports that it is true
that Jesus died naked.
And more,
the tradition of crucifixion
from the first century
also suggests that it is true.
The text makes a point of telling us
explicitly
that they stripped Jesus
and that they gave his clothing away.
And that he died alone and naked
is clearly part of the point of the story
in the Gospel of Mark.

In this Markan version
the arrest of Jesus
has an interesting twist
that can help us appreciate the importance
of how Jesus died.

It seems that the soldiers came
armed with weapons
to seize Jesus.
By itself,
this does seem a bit odd,
as Jesus himself is said to have remarked,
since he was present in the temple
almost every day,
(except probably for his day off)
teaching and healing.
They could have nabbed him any old day!

But anyway, that is how they came,
with swords and clubs,
a mean and fierce-looking band of soldiers
with Judas in the lead.
So Judas came forward,
as he'd planned to do,
and got the ball rolling
by kissing Jesus.
Immediately they laid hands on him
and seized him!
For the first time,
violent hands
were laid on the peacemaker!
And how odd
that it should have started with a kiss!
The text tells us that
all who were with him
forsook him and fled.

Were these the same ones
who had just broken bread with him?
Were these the same ones
who had been attracted enough
to Jesus
to have left their personal lives
behind them
in order to join with him?
Were these the same ones
who had been his friends?
I think they were.

But, nonetheless,
off they
ran. . . .

But here comes the twist:
one man seemed to linger,
he was a young man,
clothed only in some kind of linen cloth,
the kind in which people are baptized
. . .and buried.

The text tells us that
the soldiers seized him
but that he wriggled out of his linen cloth,
wriggled out of his baptism,
wriggled out of his call-to-death,
and fled.
But the text is explicit in making the point
that he ran off naked.
Why is this so important?

To the audience of the first century
it carried a deep meaning.

Clothing gives a person identity.
This is true today
but it was especially true
in the first century
when this text was written.
By using that symbol,
nakedness,
the writer of that story
starts redefining what it means
for Jesus
to Reign as Ruler of All.

Jesus was wrapped in swaddling clothing
on the night of his birth.
This was no accident:
the author of that text is telling us
that Jesus was earthy,
human,
poor
of the "humus."

John the Baptizer
always wore the garment of Elijah
because it best represented
the mission of his life
as the last and connecting prophet.

At the Transfiguration,
    the story tells us
    that Jesus was clothed
in a garment that showed his glory.

The young man sitting in the tomb
    after the resurrection
    wore this same white garment
    to properly announce
        Jesus' victory over death.

Paul speaks of "putting on Christ
    like a garment."

The Christian Scripture is filled
    with stories of nakedness and clothing.

Clothing made the person.
It announced to all who the person was
    what role the person would play
    and what attitude the person took.
Clothing made you somebody!
    because it identified you
    as more than nobody.
So when this young man ran away naked,
    at the time of the arrest of Jesus,
    he ran away as a nobody.
Baptism had made him somebody
    but leaving Jesus
    had made him
    a nobody.

And that Jesus died naked
    is very important;
        it is a crucial part of the story
        and helps us understand so much
        about grace
that we simply cannot continue to overlook it.

But before we explore these important
    connections
    let's examine two more stories
    about clothing in the gospels.

The first is one that will surprise you.
You will ask,
    "How is this a story about clothing?"
It is the story of the Prodigal Son.
When this runaway son came home
    to ask his father's forgiveness,
    he had a plan made
    and a speech written.
The text is in Luke's Gospel.

In his little rehearsed speech,
    the son planned to offer to return
    as a servant,
    as a slave,
    as a hired hand.
In the days when Jesus told this story,
    it would have been very clear
    to his audience
    that this would mean that
    he would not wear the clothing of a son
        because, for the most part,
        servants, especially field slaves,
        worked naked
        worked as nobodies.
The audience would have found this
    to be really something!
        The son of a landowner,
        the son of a nobleman,
        working as a servant!
        dressing as a slave!
That would really have been remarkable!

So here comes the son down the road
    with the father running out to meet him.

The kid begins his speech:
"Dad,
I know that what I've done
can never be undone
and I know that
I have broken your heart
and no longer deserve
to be called
    your son...."
But the father interrupts him.
And what does the father say?
"Quick! Get a *garment* for my son!
A ring for his finger!
Sandals for his feet!
Dress him!
Why?
Because my *son* has returned!"
To the audience of the first century,
    that said it all.

I have a question about this story:
    Is this really a story about two young people,
    the "good son" and the "prodigal son"?
        or is it,
        more to the point,
    really a story about one young man
    with two competing inner voices,
        one voice urging him
        to be at home with himself and God
        and the other urging him
        away from himself and God?
The text tells us that
    while he was away from "home"
    the young man "came to his senses"
    which means,
    I think,
        that he realized, finally,
        that he was not living
        as he was created to live,
        that he was not being his full self.

His decision to return "home"
　　was at once a decision to return to himself.
But even after he got there,
　　that other nagging voice,
　　the one of the "good son,"
　　kept him from forgiving himself.
The "good son" in us,
　　often holds more against us
　　than the "father" does.

In another place in this same gospel,
　　there is another story about clothing
　　that will help us to
　　understand even more deeply
　　how important this symbol is
　　　　for us.
In this story,
　　a "man with demons"
　　meets Jesus one day
　　　　just as Jesus is landing in a boat.
This guy,
　　the text tells us,
　　had spent years living among the tombs,
　　among the dead,
and he had worn no clothing.
He lived naked. He was nobody.

We are given to believe
　　that this guy is insane,
　　screaming awful things
　　　　and frightening the people.
The text does not say this
　　but I think it would be fair
　　to conclude
　　that all of us are insane
　　　　sometimes.
All of us are screaming inside
　　and from time to time
　　we scream outside, too.

Jesus knew how this felt;
    he had felt that way himself.
His presence to this man
    was a healing one,
    a presence that would
    "drive those demons out" of the man.
As the story goes,
    the local workers,
    frightened by all of this,
    go tell the townspeople
      who,
      as might be expected,
      rush out to see what had happened.
I can just see them coming down the road
    toward the lakefront
    where all this had taken place.
They want to know who this Jesus is
    and what happened to those demons.
When they get there,
    the text tells us,
    they found Jesus all right
    but they also found this fellow
    that Jesus had healed
      and the text is explicit in saying
      that they found him clothed
      and sitting at the feet of Jesus.
He had met the power of Jesus;
    he was no longer nobody.
    he was no longer naked;
    now he was clothed because
now he was somebody!

All of this helps us to understand
    that when Jesus was stripped
    and when he died naked
    the people were saying
      that he was nobody special to them.
And all of this helps us to understand
    one kind of nakedness in the Scriptures:
    "the nakedness of nobodiness."

This is the kind of nakedness
    that people experience often in their lives.
It is a nakedness of distortion
    sin
    rupture
    violence
    and meanness.
People who are raped
    are made naked in this way:
    the nakedness of nobodiness.
Rape,
    inside or outside of marriage,
    renders people as nobodies.
People who are victims of gossip
    are made naked in this way.
    Even when the facts being reported
        in the gossip
        are true,
still, a person is being emotionally stripped
    without his or her consent;
    they are being made naked
    as though they were nobody.
People who use others for casual sex,
    sex without commitment,
    are stripping others in this way,
even when the other gives consent to the sex.
    They are not saying to that person:
    "You are really somebody to me!"
        They are saying, instead,
        "You are nobody, really;
        I just want to have sex."
The nakedness of nobodiness is everywhere
    in our society today.

But,
    thank goodness,
    it is not the end of the story.

We're going to come back to this
in a moment,
but first,
we need to talk about another kind
of nakedness,
"the nakedness of somebodiness."

It is impossible
absolutely impossible,
even for a fundamentalist,
to read the story of creation in Genesis
and not realize that
God created the human body naked,
unclothed,
in all its glory!
The creation of the human body,
including the sexual parts,
is not the result of "the fall"
in the story.
But rather,
as Fran Ferder has pointed out,
it is the culminating high point
of all of creation!

Whether you read the story as literally true
or as symbolically relevant,
you come to the same conclusions:
the human body was God's idea.
Now get this:
rather than nakedness being the result
of "the fall"
clothing is!
It is easy to see that going naked is God's idea
while wearing clothing
is,
in a pretty significant way,
a symbol of our sinfulness.

And that's why,
>when we reach the pinnacle of love
>>with someone,
>we take off all our clothing
>and lie naked together.
We touch one another,
>marvel in one another's beauty,
>affirm one another,
>love one another deeply.
It is at these moments
>that we experience the
>>"nakedness of somebodiness."

Now we are naked
>not because we are nobody to this person,
>but because we have really become
>>somebody special
>>important
>>unique
>>individuated
>>significant
>>>and holy.
This physical nakedness is powerful,
>creative,
>and life-giving
because it is not selfish.
It is a physical nakedness
>which has been preceded by emotional nakedness.
The sharing of dreams
>ideals
>desires
>fantasies
>feelings
>and commitments
>has rendered each person
>>emotionally naked.
The physical nakedness which follows upon that
>is only natural
>because it is a symbol or expression
>of the intimacy of emotional nakedness.

This is a nakedness
that we long for
dream about having
fantasize about
and work toward.

There is a book in the Hebrew Scriptures
that tells this story better than any other.
It is the Song of Songs.
This is the story of a love affair.
It is a collection of lyric poetry
which is graceful
sensuous
and erotic
and it is included here in the Bible
because this level of nakedness
returns us to an understanding
of our primary relationship with God,
and therefore with one another,
as a relationship in which
the "nakedness of somebodiness"
is the highest form of expression.

We take off our clothes without shame
and join one another
for a moment of intimacy
that lasts for a lifetime!
And for those who do not have those moments
in which they are nakedly somebody,
you can say what you will,
there is something missing in their lives.

We are made to be somebody.

It is an interesting footnote
on this commentary
that in some Christian churches,
readings from the Song of Songs are omitted
from the regular cycle of liturgical texts,
presumably because they are so erotic!

In the Roman lectionary,
these texts are included
only for the feast of St. Mary Magdalene
who was thought to be a prostitute!
(A careful reading of Scripture,
by the way,
does not support that thought.)
But what are we saying as a church by suggesting
even indirectly,
that being erotic is material
only for reformed prostitutes?
The exclusion of these texts
and the general exclusion of preaching
on love and love-making
have to be a starting point for us
now as we continue
to consider grace and nakedness.

You see,
Jesus,
when he was hanging there
naked on the cross,
took the nakedness of nobodiness
with which they intended to kill him,
and transformed it
into the nakedness of somebodiness.
In doing this,
Jesus undid
what had happened in the story of the garden
in the Book of Genesis.

There they were naked, of course,
until their relationship with God
was ruptured by selfishness:
they'd treated God as a nobody.
Then their nakedness became
a source of shame.

But Jesus,
    naked and hanging there for the world to see
    took that shame,
        that selfishness,
        that nobodiness,
    and made it into something entirely different.

This is such an important point
    that I honestly don't see
    how we can understand
    the life and death of Jesus
without exploring it a little further.

On the cross,
in the midst of violence
    rejection
    hatred
    abuse
    ridicule
    and apparent failure
(all the stuff of which nobodies are made)
Jesus responded with forgiveness.

He took the opposite action.
    We should not be surprised
        to hear this.
After all,
    this is the same Jesus
    who,
    time after time,
        confused the crowds
        (and us)
    by teaching that
    we must die in order to live
    must give in order to receive
    must be weak in order to be strong.
Now he is teaching us
    that we must forgive,
    in order to end violence,
        the violence
that creates the nakedness of nobodiness.

Now,
when you hear the word "forgiveness"
    if you are a Catholic,
    and probably even if you aren't,
    you likely think of confession
        where people used to go
        to "get forgiveness"
    (which was a pastoral abuse,
not a theological position of the church).

Try to forget that connection.
    Forgiveness,
    Jim Lopresti has said,
happens *before* the sin, not after it.
It is a "givenness before."
    It is a permanent attitude.
    It is an unconditional positioning
        of one person toward another.
Confession was never anything more
    than the celebration of that fact
    that we were *already forgiven* by God!

Jesus forgave them,
    which is to say that he
    gave up any claims that he had on them
    for the pain
        embarrassment
        false charges
        and even death
            that they caused him.
He gave up his claims on them,
    which means that
    he held nothing against them,
which is the key part of forgiveness.

Jesus' forgiveness of them
    was a powerful,
    creative act.

Pilate once told Jesus,
    "Don't you know that I have the power
        to free you
        or the power to have you killed."
Jesus responded: "You have no power over me."

When Jesus said that,
    this is what he was talking about.
By forgiving them,
    Jesus gave them no power.
Even as they were acting,
    even as they were exercising their "power,"
    Jesus was talking it all away from them
    was rendering them powerless.
What could they do to him?

In doing this,
Jesus was saying that God
    had no claims on us, either.
For God,
the first exercise of power was in creation:
    the creation of the human person,
    the energizing of human persons with life,
    and the energizing of the world with Spirit.
And the second exercise of power for God
    was in donating this creation
    to us,
    especially in the person of Jesus,
        his ownmost self,
        now present with us.
It's amazing when you think of it
    that God would not have hung on
    to all that had been created.
But God made absolutely no claims on creation,
    giving it all to us.
God gave up all claims
    even on the human family,
    rightful though those claims
    would have been.

That is,
God gave up God's own rightful claims on Creation,
    gave humans their freedom
        to live
        to love
    and to listen to God as they want.

So Jesus,
    in giving up his rightful claims on the cross,
    transformed nakedness.
Now,
    rather than being a naked nobody,
    Jesus was a naked somebody
        because he was loving us
    with the kind of love that lovers know.
He was expressing total vulnerability
    total unconditionality
    total presence.
There has been no more dramatic
    expression of love
    in the history of the world!

And Jesus' own great act of forgiveness
    has freed us
    and has procreated in us
    the power for forgiveness
which is the power to transform the world.

For us this is grace:
We spoke already about the power
    to be our ownmost selves.

Now we are speaking about the power
that comes from Jesus' word of forgiveness:
    When you are stripped by gossip: forgive.
    When you are violated by rape: forgive.
    When you are victimized by violence: forgive.
    When you are stunned by murder: forgive.
    When you are an object of lust: forgive.

When you are hurt
    rejected
    ridiculed
    spat upon
or even killed: forgive.
Do not give your enemies power over you
    by holding claims against them.
Forgive the oppressors,
    forgive the racists
    forgive the sexists
    forgive the communists
    forgive them all!

This is the mystery of the cross for us:
    Jesus says on that cross:
"Do you think this will keep me
    from loving you?
        Do you?
Do you think this'll stop me?"

It's really very impractical,
    forgiveness is.
If you forgive,
    you'll be done in for sure.
But that's the point:
    if getting done in doesn't bother you,
    then what have you got to lose?
What's left to hurt you?
You will then have absolute freedom.

Now, a footnote:
Here's a dire warning:
    this does not mean that
    we are ever excused from working
for Peace and Justice in the world.

By describing one who forgives,
    we are not describing one who is passive
    in the face of oppression
        violence
        and evil.

There is a great misunderstanding
    about the death of Jesus
    that floats about
    certain religious circles
        from time to time.
Some people believe
    that Jesus was simply
        passive
    in allowing himself to be killed.
This notion comes from
    a mistaken view
    of the humanity of Jesus.
Jesus was fully human;
    he did not,
    from time to time wander
    between humanity and divinity.
He was full of the energy of grace,
    which enabled and empowered him
    to live his full life,
    which is the life of God,
    but he did not exercise
        this power unilaterally.
That was his point.

Don't you remember the taunting
    of the soldiers,
"If you are really God,
    come down from that cross"?
By believing that Jesus
    could have stopped the killers
    if he'd only wanted to,
        we participate in that taunting!
Jesus could not have stopped them:
    he was fully human.

What Jesus did in that moment
    was far from passive!
Yet, there are those who believe
    that somehow being passive
    in the face of suffering
    would be acceptable in our day.

These believe that
    by suffering silently like that
    a person can identify
    most closely with
        the suffering of Jesus.
"You should accept suffering,"
    these would say,
    "because that suffering
        identifies you with Jesus."

But no,
we would say, based on this understanding
    of Jesus and Grace,
    that we do not have to suffer
        any longer
        because of the suffering of Christ!

Just consider the overall tone of the gospels,
    and of the approach of Jesus,
    was to do everything that is humanly possible,
    empowered with the love of God,
    to remedy evil.

We are not called to be passive
    in the face of injustice.
Quite the contrary,
    we are obliged to
    carry one another's burdens
    bear one another's sorrows
and provide for one another's needs.

And for those
    whose claims have been systematically
    taken away by others,
    we must work to restore them at once!
There is no mistaking it.

Let's return now to our central
    line of thinking in this chapter:
All of us are victims
    of nobodiness.

All of us are rendered naked
    by insensitive or evil persons
    over whose actions we do not
        always have control.
All of us have run off to be wanton,
    like the prodigal child in the story.
All of us are slaves sometimes,
    choosing to be nobody or to make
    somebody else into a nobody
    for our supposed benefit.
But more,
all of us want to be naked with somebody.

We want it
because we are born
to be in union like that.

But,
so often,
    the only nakedness we experience
    is the nakedness of nobodiness.
How can we transform that?
    The lesson
    is the one we've just learned
    from Jesus' own transformation.
Because, for all of us,
    all of us,
    the power of forgiveness
    can restore us,
    can remake us
    can reconcile us
and we can become somebody again!

6

GRACE IS ORDINARY

I think it was Will Rogers
    who once said that
    life is just one damn thing after another.
We want to talk about that next.
People live their lives every day.
On the face of it,
    that may seem like kind of
    an obvious thing to say.
But think about it for a minute:
    our lives are filled with commonness
        with ordinariness
        with repetition
        with mundane earthiness
        with everydayness.
We live every day:
    we get up
    we get through the bathroom routine
    we get a bite to eat
    we get on with the tasks of the day
    we get back to work
    we get finished
    we get to supper
    we get some time in the evening
    we get to bed.

In the midst of all this,
How are we supposed to see the Glory of God
every day?

How are we supposed to recognize
the grace and power of God
every day?

How on earth are we supposed to recognize
the Reign of God
as it breaks into our lives
every day?

An important question, this,
and the one on our minds in this chapter.
The answer is not easy,
and not easy to put into words.
But putting it into words
is exactly the way to understanding it.
Some folks would say
that daily Mass
regular prayer times
spiritual direction
joining a prayer group
volunteering in the parish
or having holy cards around the house
are the ways to recognize
The Reign of God
The In-breaking of the Holy Spirit
The Presence of the Risen One
in their lives.
But it is possible,
no, it is probable,
that if we are busy
with all of those other things
we will miss it completely.
I mean to say exactly what I said.

If we stay busy
    with activity
    with parish duties
    with busy-ness
    we will miss seeing God.
The church can be an obstacle to grace,
    as well as a moment of grace.

In order to recognize the grace we speak of here,
    we must step back from programs
        structures
        organizations
        and hierarchies,
    in a word, from churchiness.
We need to step back
    in order to gain perspective
    on things spiritual.
We need to step back
    in order not to take
    too much for granted
    in this constantly surprising
        part of our lives.
We need to step back
    in order to forget ourselves.
The kind of experience of grace
    that we will talk about here
    is one,
        after all,
        that even the unchurched have
        on a very regular basis
    and that often the most churched
        miss completely.

So we're not talking here
    only about people who come to Mass,
    only about people who say their prayers,
    only about church "insiders,"
    or only about "faithful" Catholics.

We're talking as well
    about all those others
    who also experience God in their lives,
        even when they don't call it that
        or even when they don't admit that.
We're also talking
    about those parts of life
    that sometimes seem remote from God,
    those parts
    that don't seem to have anything
        to do
        with the traditional ways that
        we have come to understand the
            work of God in our lives.

So where do we start?
We start with God: Where is God?
    "What kind of question is that?"
        you might ask.
    "We all know where God is, don't we?"
        But do we?
We have always been taught that God is "out there"
    wherever that is,
    or we've been taught that
God's in heaven and all's well with the world.

We carry around inside of us
    (even those of us
    who think a lot about God do this)
we carry around a sense that God is distant
    absent
    busy
    and uninvolved.
We have a sense that
        when it comes to real life,
        to everyday living,
    Our God is an "outsider god."

It's surprising to us to realize this,
   even those of us who think we know God,
   even those of us who refuse to admit
         that this is true,
   even those of us who look upon
   the unchurched and are grateful
         that we "aren't like the rest of them..."
   many of us treat God this way,
   as though God were outside of us.

But nothing could be farther from the truth.
And this belief,
   that our God is an outsider god,
   which the church itself
   has had a large hand
   in forming as a popular belief,
this belief is one major source of pain
         suffering
         sickness
         alienation
         and division.

We must do all we can to move forward,
   to grow in our understanding,
   but more important,
   to grow in our experience,
of the God who is an *insider* in our lives.

How can we do this?

The key approach
   to take
   for the one who wants to live with God
   is to listen.
Listen to what?

We go along in our lives,
   living every day
   in a willy-nilly sort of way.

We don't think much about
    our common tasks
    ideas
    conversations
    or events.
They all just sort of happen,
       day in and day out,
       one thing after another.
And we talk about
      this stuff that goes on in our lives
      in the same, common way:
    "No big deal,"
    "we did this," we say,
      "or we did that today."
    "This came to pass,
      or that didn't," we might say to someone.
We talk about
    the everyday, common stuff of our lives
    with an everyday, common language,
      nothing fancy,
      just plain old words.

But,
every now and then,
    sometimes every day,
    or even several times per day,
those plain old words just don't do it.
Then you hear us say,
    "I just can't tell you how much…"
      or
    "Words just can't describe how I feel…"
      or
    "There's no way I could tell you…"

And we mean precisely what we are saying:
    we've run out of language,
    run out of the words we need
      to describe certain experiences
      in our lives.

It's as though we've come to the end
of words.
Plain words can no longer explain
the experience
or express
the feelings.
We are simply left speechless by whatever happened.

What causes this?
Maybe a sunrise.
Maybe a warm expression of affection
from someone.
Maybe an overwhelming, spontaneous
sense of well-being.
Maybe a death, or a birth.
Maybe news of an illness.
Maybe a phone call from an old friend.
Maybe the afterglow of sexual loving.
Many experiences may cause this
speechlessness.

These experiences are no longer ordinary,
common, everyday experiences for us.
Because we notice them
in a special,
observant way,
they begin to take on
new meaning.
They become full of meaning for us.
We begin to identify these experiences
as important,
as unique to us:
we begin to see that they are
what makes us truly human.
They are no longer
simply raw human experiences,
undefined and unrefined,
but now they are dignified
lived
and wholly us.

We load them up
    with meaning and significance
    and they quickly and importantly
        become the stuff
        of which our memories are made.
Later we find
    when we are in other related moments
    that we do certain things
        as though "in memory" of them.
We memorialize these moments
    and re-celebrate them again and again.

These moments or events
    become very special to us then;
    so special, in fact,
        that we are left speechless
        in the face of them:
    They are too beautiful
        terrible
        mysterious
        lovely
        peaceful
        wonderful
        frightening
        tremendous
        and alluring
to ever adequately be described
            in mere words.

They push us to our outer limits,
    to the edge of the ordinary,
    to our boundaries,
    to our deepest depths.
We aren't sure how to respond,
        how to talk or act.

We can't explain how we feel
    because the ordinary language
    is not sufficient.
But who has a language that is sufficient?

We are tempted to go to a scientist
        (they know everything, you know).
    But we would not ask a scientist
            to describe love to us
            because,
    while their explanation might be accurate,
        scientifically speaking,
        it would not be loving.
No.
To describe love,
        we would ask a poet
            an artist
            a painter
            a sculptor
            or a music writer.
But the language of the poet
is not ordinary, common language to us.
It is a language that seems to come
        from the other side.

The other side?

Yes,
the other side.
We are beginning to speak now about God,
        that one who is on the Other Side.
        But we must be careful to note
                that, while God is on the Other Side,
                God is not,
                thereby,
                        on the outside.

When we finally face the fact
        that we've gone beyond the ordinary,
        we stand at the edge of what we know
        and can control,
    and we peer over that edge into the unknown;
            and we ask,
                sometimes we shout,
            the Ultimate Questions:

What is over there?
Do we dare to go there?
Will we find there some way
    to express our depths?
Will this give meaning to our lives?
Can we endure?
What does all this mean?
Is anyone there?
What the hell is going on?
(Trite as these may sometimes seem,
    they are the Ultimate Questions.)

So we stand at the edge,
    peering over into the darkness,
    feeling at once lured beyond
    yet frightened to go there.

These are very key moments in our lives
    and they happen with frequency,
    although not always with the same force.
These are moments of decision
    moments of grace.
These are *the* moments of grace in our lives.

It is as though
    we face our true selves
    in these moments,
    our full and true selves
and we gather all of that self together,
gather in the rough and the smooth,
    and have the opportunity,
    an opportunity offered to everyone,
        to be transformed
        to be moved
        to be transfixed
        to be made whole:
and therefore to be made holy.

Let me remind you:
    these are not usually moments
    that can be scheduled
    in the parish bulletin.

They are moments, rather,
    that catch us
    grip us
    hold us
    almost beg us to take notice
        and thereby be moved beyond.

The trick,
    we began here by saying,
    is to listen for them.
By using the word "listen" here
    we mean to say
    that we need to pause,
    often,
    in the daily on-goings of life,
    pause to reflect
    on what is going on:
        the person who called by phone
        the letter we received today
        the beauty that is rushing past
            our car windows
        the people we are meeting on the streets
        the kiss we received and gave this
            morning
        the illness we are experiencing today
        that article in the news about that child,
        this or that,
all stuff from our everyday lives:
    we need to pause to notice it,
    reflect on it,
    let it touch us,
    let it move us.

This really isn't very complicated:
For example,
    you go to lunch with a friend,
    but instead of talking
    only about "the weather"
        instead of chattering about nothing
        you talk about what's really going on.

You explore your life.
You ask tough questions.
You ask the ultimate questions.

What you have when you do this,
    is a moment of grace.
    What began as lunch,
        can end as eucharist
        or reconciliation
        or healing
    or whatever you call it.

Only when we are touched and moved
    by the everyday events and people
    of our lives,
        can we be touched and moved
        by God,
    whoever he or she may be.

That is why the busy-ness of our lives,
    and often of the church,
    can be an obstacle,
    a defense mechanism
        against the honesty
        intimacy
        and holiness
    of crossing over and moving beyond
    the ordinary.

You see,
    as we stand on that awe-full edge,
    peering over to the Other Side,
    we must make a terrible choice.

No one and nothing
can ever force us to move beyond that edge.
We must choose to do it.

The choice,
    the terrible choice, then,
    is to go beyond or to turn back.

Many of us will turn back.
We turn to cope the best we can
    and we invent ways to make that coping
        possible for us.
    We may use alcohol to cope
        or drugs
        or meaningless sex
        or work
        or busy-ness
        or intellectualism
        or consumerism
        or partying
        or "macho-ism"
        or eating.
We turn back to lose ourselves
    in compulsion
    rather than move forward
    to find ourselves on the Other Side.
The turning back becomes a habit,
    some would say a religion.
By turning back,
    we pass through the same experiences
    of self-discovery
    sexual discovery
    death or birth
    beauty
    horror
    pain
    or wonder
but instead of being led to Meaning by them,
        we turn around in fear
        and do not reflect on them
        do not allow them to form us
        do not admit our feelings
        do not share them with others
        do not come out into the open
            but rather we hide.

Sometimes we are afraid:
    Others will think that we
        "just couldn't handle it."
    We don't want to appear to be a fool,
        or worse,
        a weakling.
We don't want to appear dependent on anyone,
        or needy
        or confused
        or, and here's the key: vulnerable.
So instead,
    we bury it all inside ourselves
        and try to go on
        as though nothing had happened.
What fools we can be!

We can never just go on.
    We are constantly changed.
    We are always being formed.

So as we stand at the edge,
    the other choice,
    the opportunity we have,
    is to give meaning to the stuff of life
        by leaping into
        what is apparently darkness
        but, we discover,
        is really Light.
We do that
    by embracing these experiences,
    admitting the feelings
    sharing ourselves with others
    dealing with the joy and pain
    and finding,
        on the Other Side,
        the language
to adequately describe all of that,
and, therefore,
    to own it
    and to let it become a part of ourselves.

In short,
    we cross over by telling our story
    and by letting our stories
    be made meaningful as they're shared among others.

You see,
we can't share alone.
    We know that we can't
    we know that we don't have the words.
But we can find the words,
    the language we need,
    on the Other Side.
And there have been people
    telling their stories like this
    for centuries.
We are certainly never alone
    as we struggle to find words
    to describe our experiences.
We are not alone.
We have,
    for starters,
    the authors of the letters and gospels.
    We have the early mothers and fathers:
        the stories of faith
        from then until now.
But we also have
    our neighbors
    friends
    family
    and even strangers
        who appear in our midst.
We have to become vulnerable,
    we have to admit our story is true:
        I am sick.
        I am so happy!
        I am weak in faith.
        I need friendship.
        I am grateful.

I am gay.
I don't want children.
I love you so much.
I am alcoholic.
I am who I am.
Does that sound familiar?
It is
and it is the beginning of
finding a language
to adequately describe ourselves,
our Word.

This language of the Other Side
is not ordinary.
It is transcendent:
two people sharing
poetry
all kinds of music
wedding dances
painting
silence
touch
imagination
crying and tears
truth-telling
a whole theater of language
that gives a way to express meaning
and that,
all taken together,
is called religious language
(which is not the same as churchy language).

There is a strange and powerful mystery in this:
in order to cross over,
thereby encountering the Other,
whom we name God,
we must give up ourselves.

There is a kind of dying we must do
    as we stand at that edge, peering over.
We give up our ordinary self
    in order to receive in return
    a transformed Self.
This dying is the key.
Unless we are willing to
    die to ourselves,
we should not expect to find this new life.

It is a strange mystery
    and mystery is incomprehensible:
    that is its nature.
This cannot be explained:
    it can be pointed to,
    we can build ritual around it,
    we can probe it theologically,
    but, ultimately,
        it remains mystery.

So we don't know why we must die,
we only know we must.

But what does this mean?
    "to die...."
It means, really,
    that we become vulnerable,
    we become open
    we stop the hiding and lying
    we face the truth once and for all
    we let go the controls.
Dying like this is very scary business.
We are both drawn to it,
    yet frightened of it.

Dying usually begins with denial:
    we deny the truth
    just as Peter did at the trial.
Then it moves to anger,
    we know the truth but
    we are angry that it is the truth,
    just as Peter became angry at the trial.

Soon we begin to bargain
   accepting the truth,
   but with our own conditions attached.
Until we begin to see that we are who we are
   and then we grasp
   the sheets of our deathbed
   clinging desperately,
   hoping not to have to pass through this.
But finally, we let go,
   we become vulnerable
   we open ourselves up
   we begin to talk about ourselves
     and then
     we find ourselves
       strangely,
       mysteriously,
       but undeniably
       at peace....
This can happen
in the Sacrament of Reconciliation
   but it also happens,
   more often,
     over lunch with a friend,
     talking with a child,
     a phone call in the night,
     pillow talk
     boat talk
     and other common ways of
   coming to grips with ourselves.

This is how God speaks to us,
   not many words,
     as Brian McDermott has said,
   but one basic word,
   a word divinely spoken,
   and that word is nothing less
   than the life of the one
   who prays in this way,
     that life as continually
     drawn into God.

Listening to God
　　in this way
　　means listening to our lives
　　as lives being drawn into God
　　all the time....
We become now, not a word,
　　but rather a Word
　　spoken by God.

Notice this:
It isn't that God operates from outside of us,
　　controlling us like a puppet,
　　but rather that our very Self
　　　　is transformed
　　by the encounter with these new words,
　　this new dying,
　　this new language,
this Word of God.

Our Self is transformed now
　　so that even the ordinary
　　to which we return
　　and in which we live
will never be the same again!

This whole, simple process
　　of naming our experiences in life,
　　of coming to the edge,
　　of facing the ultimate questions,
　　of choosing to turn back or go beyond
　　is something we often face alone.
But for those who choose to move beyond
　　for those who choose to die to self,
　　this journey
　　　　to the heart of the Lord
　　　　will not ever be traveled alone.
And this is our point here:
　　we are graced,
　　everyone is graced,
　　　　empowered, in other words,
　　　　to move beyond and be transformed.

And the grace is communicated to us
in the community
which is the Body of Christ.

This is such a powerful reality
that we can scarcely scratch its surface
in attempting to describe it here.
But this much is very clear:
we must bring ourselves to each other,
wounded or rejoicing,
vulnerable in any case,
bring ourselves to each other,
giving ourselves away
in intimacy
trust
and faith.
What we receive back
will be our full
transformed
whole and Holy Self.

7

GRACE AND SIN

Let's not kid ourselves:
in order to understand grace
we've got to talk about sin.
Most of us
were taught as children that sin
was how we would lost grace.
Certain very serious sins
could, in fact,
knock us out of the running
for the Kingdom of Heaven.
That was a sort of
whittling away that sin did
on our souls:
too many little sins,
and our otherwise pure souls
would be sprinkled with sins
until the purity was gone
and we were in serious trouble with God.

Sin was the opposite of grace.
When someone asked forgiveness for sins,
grace was restored.
There was a great deal of popular piety
about sin.

We need to talk about sin
  because, for the most part,
  the truths contained in how we were taught
  are still the same truths
    but how we understand
    the dynamics of sin
      has changed very much.

So we will talk for a bit about sin
  but if you are someone who wants
  to understand sin as it relates to
  the laws of the church,
skip this chapter and move to Leviticus.
The norm we will use here
  will not be the law.
As we will see,
  we can sometimes follow the law to its letter,
  and still commit serious sin.
Following the law,
  as Jesus pointed out many times,
  is no sure way to seek the Lord.
Seeking the Lord means seeking the Truth.
Seeking the truth means examining the heart,
    and examining the heart
    will sometimes support the law
    but will sometimes challenge the law.

Our norm here,
for this examination of conscience,
  will be human authenticity.
We have seen repeatedly what that means:
    To be authentic
    is to be all that we are created to be.
The created self
  is not self-made
  self-determined or
  self-centered.
The created self
  is a self-for-others
  self-with-earth
  self-open-unto-mystery.

The question must always be:
"Is this act
    judgment
    attitude
    motive,
is it really *me*?"
We don't mean here a me centered on me,
    but a created me,
    centered, therefore, in mystery
    and discovered in relationship
        to others and the earth.

To be human is to be graced,
    we have said.
This means that we all receive
    God, revealing god-self to us.
That is,
    we have an energy
    of self-understanding:
        we can, in short,
        know and possess ourselves.
We also can communicate ourselves
    to others.
In fact,
    it is in our very nature to do so.
Likewise, we can receive
    the self-communication of Holy Mystery,
    whom we have named God.
And we can also know the transcendent
    moving beyond our human experience
        into Great and Holy Mystery.

All of this forms our movement into Mystery,
    our search for God.
But this search for God is ambiguous.
We live, after all,
    in a world that is a mixture
    of both grace and sin.

There is light
  but there is also darkness:
    systems that oppress people
    unjust structures
    temptations to live for ourselves
    subtle manipulation in intimacy
    insensitivity
    destructive competition
    escapism
    compulsion
    dishonesty.

This will be an examination of conscience,
  and it will,
  in a powerful way,
summarize all that we've said here about grace.

The "letter of the law" approach
  to sin and grace
  has gotten us into some trouble.
We've forgotten to seek authenticity
  which is much more difficult
  than keeping the letter of the law.
But it would not be possible for you
  to show me in Scripture
  where it was ever suggested,
    even remotely,
    that keeping the letter of the law
would somehow be enough for the followers of Jesus.
If I read the text correctly,
  the very opposite is true:
    the law is a guide
    and can sometimes be helpful
    but it is by no means
    all there is.
By no means. There is much more.

It is that "much more"
  that we will examine here.
Now, it isn't possible to cover everything
  in one volume on grace and sin,
  but we can begin.

What we will do here is
   choose several central areas
   and stay with those,
   developing them as an example
   of a way to apply what we've said
     about grace.
You can do the rest on your own.

Let's start by talking about Sunday.
   Remember Sunday?
The letter of the law
   tells us that we should get to church
   on Sunday.
But getting to church
   in no way fulfills our "obligation."
There have been two extremes with this:
   those who fulfill the minimal obligation
   and those who insist that nothing else
   should be done that day but formal prayer.
Neither is right.
We live our lives in time,
   running always against the clock.
We also live our lives on a finite earth,
   working against gravity
   needing to fix up our space.

Our lives are full of cares
   for food, shelter, pleasures.
We spend our time,
   so much of it,
   planning to buy and buying
   that sometimes
   it seems
     we run into a wall
     unable to relax
     unable to let go
   controlled by the demands of time
   and the need to fix our space.

Sunday puts an end to all of that.
It floats somewhere outside of time:
   we needn't keep schedules on Sunday.
And it floats somewhere outside of space:
   our cares can be suspended for one day,
      can't they?
We need a day to float
   and Sunday is that day.
Keeping holy the Sabbath means letting go of cares.
It means having time to do things that we
   normally would not:
      visiting family
      calling on the neighbors
      taking a nap
      sitting around
   in a word, killing time.
Not a bad idea, that,
   for people as concerned
   with time as we are.
Sunday is a Holy Pause,
   and not to have paused
   is not to have kept holy the Sabbath,
      no matter how many times
      you've been to church.
And it is all of this pausing
   that gives us time for reflection
   on how we live the rest of our lives.

Let's talk now
   about other times of prayer.
When we were children,
   we were probably taught that it was a sin
   to miss our daily prayers.
I think that's true.
We've said earlier here
   that taking several Holy Pauses each day
   would allow us to find ourselves
   in the revealing presence of
      Holy Mystery.

The failure to pause will drive us away from
    ourselves,
    it will prevent us from being authentic,
    and therefore, it is sinful.
I think this is among the most serious sins
    it is possible for us to commit.
It is much more serious than
    the traditional "bad" sins:
        those against purity.

Moving on,
this is a tough one:
Whatever serves as our ultimate goal
    becomes our god.
for many of us,
    that ultimate goal,
    often sleeping beneath the surface,
    unwilling to rear its ugly head,
    difficult for us to admit,
    embarrassing when it appears,
        is materialism.
There is little in human experience
    more captivating.
We have,
    buried within our human spirit,
    a constant desire for "more."
By itself, there is nothing wrong with that.
In the story of the garden in Genesis,
    the people had all they could have wanted:
        food,
        a place to live,
        companionship,
        life with God.
What else is there really?
But they wanted more.

And the drive for more, drove them eventually away
    from themselves
    from each other,
    and, therefore,
        away from God's presence.

The very trait of human experience
   described in that story
   is the one that keeps most of us
   from ever seriously
     following Jesus.
We hate to admit this,
   but we know it's true.
This human desire for more,
   mistaken as a desire for more stuff,
   is really a desire
     for more authenticity
     more companionship
     more intimacy
     more love and laughter
     more kindness
     more peace
more of our full, created Selves.

And the thing about this is
   that the authentic "more"
   which we really seek
     is very close to us.
It is the Kingdom
   which is actually within us.

I don't know how we will ever change this next one.
We have been taught,
   somehow
   by someone invisible,
that it is always wrong to be vulnerable.
Yet personal vulnerability
   is the key to sexual loving
   and intimate human fulfillment.
Now, as I begin to talk about sex,
   I need to define this.
I'm really not sure what "having sex" means.
It is not a purely physical act,
   having sex isn't,
   because that physical act
   is an expression of a much deeper reality.

So,
when we speak of having sex,
    we mean the larger reality
    which includes the intimacy,
    the sharing of time and space,
    the common possessions,
    the joy of foreplay and intercourse
    the gaze of love,
    the long talks and walks,
    the mutual other-centeredness
and so on....
But to speak of having sex in this way
    is to suggest that each of the persons
    is vulnerable to the other.
Scripture often refers to having sex
    as a "being known" by one another.
That being known is very close to the
    reality we are describing here.
To be known
    is to be exposed
    to be open
    to take risks
    to be honest, completely honest,
    in a word, to be known is to be naked.

The spiritual nakedness that two people share,
    the spiritual and psychological vulnerability,
    is what gives way
        and gives meaning
            to physical nakedness.
It's what gives "having sex" its meaning.

This nakedness,
    this vulnerability,
    this is our most true Self,
        our created and creating Self.
In the creation story of Genesis,
    it was the crowning high point
    of all that God had done,
    and we can easily see why.

So anytime we have sex without that vulnerability,
    we are in danger of losing ourselves
    which is sin.
Fornication with strangers
    leaves us invulnerable: we may not even
    know each other's names.
Masturbation alone requires no risks,
    not even the risk of pleasures shared.
Rape makes only one person vulnerable,
    and in a completely inappropriate way.
Adultery trespasses a bond,
    creating a unilateral vulnerability
    rather than a mutual one.
Manipulative intercourse
    or intercourse used to punish
    even in marriage,
    removes the vulnerability
        and places one in power over the other.
Prostitution sets up a transaction
    in which no one is vulnerable
    to anyone
    although both are vulnerable
        to pain.
Seduction allows a person
    to guard his or her vulnerability
    while another is exposed.
Promiscuity seals a person
    in invulnerability
    allowing no opportunity for
    any kind of relationship whatsoever.
Pornography institutionalizes invulnerability,
    making it hard, cast in concrete,
    impenetrable.

People having sex together
    is a great and noble thing.
The question to ask:
    "Is this really me? Is this really us?
    Are we really being the people
    we are created to be?"

The final area of sin we will consider
  is one that can cause pain for many.
Some people are in the habit
  of denying who they are.
They make this denial
  usually out of fear
  that to admit who they are
  would bring great ruin upon them.
Sometimes they are right.
One such group is homosexuals:
  gay men and lesbians.
  They deny their attractions.
Women often deny their strength,
  their power
  their aggression.
Men deny their fragility,
  their tenderness,
  their tears.
Blue collar workers often deny
  their nobility.
The rich deny the injustice
  of their wealth
While the poor deny
  their role in impoverishment.
There are other groups as well:
  people of all types.
Denying one's created nature,
  living outside of one's true and honest self,
  makes it almost impossible
  to be the persons we are created to be.
Denying who we are
  leads to self-hate
  and makes our accusers appear right.
Denying who we are
  sets up a situation in which
  we may never know love.
We must find ways to admit who we are,
  and we must give one another the context
  in which to do that.

Sin,
we have seen,
is what keeps us away from ourselves.

It is what keeps us from living out
    our created purpose.
But, as we have also seen here,
    we are empowered to move beyond sin
    and moving beyond sin,
    which is to live
        under the enlightenment of Christ,
        will make us whole.

8

THE PRAYER OF GRACE

Something that I think is becoming clear
in this writing
is that grace is all around us;
it is easy to get,
and it is available to everyone.
It is God communicating God-self to us.
And we hear this Word of God,
this self-communication,
through everyday events and words.
When we pause
to hear this Word,
we find that it is present
in the very ordinary stuff of life.
But, beset with sin,
which is also part and parcel
of living in the world,
and which prevents us from
completely hearing the Word,
we struggle to hear:
the shouting of our hearts
can be so loud!
And, since we cannot always hear,
it is sometimes very difficult for us
to be who we are created to be.
But we struggle with the power of grace

as the engine that hums deep within us,
giving us more than enough energy
to go on,
to become our true selves.
If anything is clear here,
it is that this movement of grace
in our lives
and in the life of the community,
does not wait to be scheduled
in a parish bulletin
or a sacramental program.
(It might be sustained by the parish
with its schedule of sacraments,
but that same parish
could also prevent grace from working.)
One way to summarize what we are saying here
is to say,
simply,
that grace is natural.
Prayer comes naturally to us in this same way.
Prayer is not an ideal
which is outside of us,
something to be achieved.
It is an integral part of being human:
we are naturally oriented to prayer.
Our awareness of ourselves
others
the earth
and God
comes from our ability to reflect
and pray.
We have an inborn hunger for God.

My question is this:
if prayer is so fundamental to being human,
Why do we make it seem so difficult?
Why do we make it such a far-off goal?
Why do we complicate it with so much argument?

The language and images of the church
do not always help.

We are caught somewhat
with a church that has changed very little
in a world
which has changed a great deal.
In the language of the church,
we summon God
as though God were not already here.
"Come holy spirit..." we say.
"Our Father in Heaven..."
"Come, Lord Jesus, come..."
The God of these prayers
must be somewhere else
or we would not have to call him or her,
would we?
The buildings, too,
reach their spires into the skies,
suggesting that God is somewhere out there.
But we know that isn't true.
The words are given to Jesus, himself,
that the kingdom of heaven
is within us.
"Do not go looking here or there,"
the text says.

We do not need to call God
to come to us from somewhere outside of us.
Rather, we need to ask for
the grace of perception,
of spiritual insight,
so that we would be able to see
that we are
fundamentally oriented
and already journeying
toward this Holy Mystery
which we have named "God."

The prayer of grace, then,
is not a climbing out of ourselves to God;

it is not a leaving of ourselves behind
in order to move into God,
but rather it is a falling back
to our very Center.
The prayer of grace
does not make us more divine:
it makes us more human.

More human?
Yes. More human. Remember that Jesus
tempted in the desert
was not tempted to act like a human.
He was tempted there to forsake his humanity
and act like God:
"Turn these stones into bread."
"Throw yourself down
and let the angels bear you."
He was tempted
to abandon the truth that he'd come to reveal,
namely,
that being fully and authentically human
actualizes the potential planted within us
at creation.
Jesus did not enter the world
in order to make us all into gods.
No.
He entered the world
in order to make us all into more human Humans.

Being human,
after all,
is how we were created.
Remember the text which says
that Jesus did not deem equality with God
something to be grasped at
but rather that he became human,
being born one of us.
And it was when he accepted that which
perhaps makes us most human: death,
that God highly exalted him.

We should never pray,
   therefore,
   to be less human.
We should pray, instead,
   to be made more human,
   more fully who we are created to be.
And reflection on that creation
   is a very high form of prayer indeed.

It seems more comforting to pray to God in all
   God's Glory!
It seems to lift us out of the mundane,
   out of the ordinary,
   out of the everydayness of life.
But, like it or not,
   God chose to make the earth a place of Glory.
This is how God chose to express God-self.
This is it; this is all there is.
   And this is plenty!

So we will not find God
   by escaping the earth.
Rather than looking outside of ourselves
   or our world,
   we need to look within
   to find what we want.
The heart of the Lord can be discovered
   and visited
      only through our own hearts.
In prayer,
   we gather up all the pieces
   of our often-fragmented existence
   and we hold them consciously
   in order to gain a still point,
      a focus:
         the *heart*.
This is the place where God dwells.
   "The kingdom is not here or there:
      No,
   the kingdom is
      within you."

Jesus' own center,
    his still point,
    his own heart,
    was completely in the one he called Father,
        which was why he could so easily
        see God.
Our heart
    must also rest in the one we know
    as Father or Mother,
    as Creator,
    as Force of Life.

We need to pray, then,
    the prayer of grace:
    a prayer of acceptance
    and conversion.
Basil Pennington has helped us to see that
what is needed for us to pray in this way
    are three things only:
        a desire to be with God
        a lonely place
        and a quiet heart.

We are so uncomfortable with silence,
    though,
    that we keep an interior
    noise going,
    stimulated by exterior events,
    all of which prevent us from hearing
the stirrings of our hearts.
We are unwilling to Pause,
    unwilling to listen,
    but, until we do,
        say what you will,
        we will not
        discover the
        Heart of the Lord.
Why do we fear prayer?
    We fear it
    because we know that,
    if we really ever moved to our Center,
    if we really ever encountered the Lord there,

we would also,
simultaneously,
encounter ourselves.
We fear that we will find ourselves
somehow ugly
unlovable
incapable.
We have so accepted the ideal person
presented in modern times
in advertising and the media,
that we cannot bear to see our real selves,
full of scars,
pimples,
fears,
and, in general,
full of humanness.
Like the couple in the story of the Garden
at creation,
we don't want to be just human;
we think it would be better to be God.
But this is the point:
It's great to be human!
Even God is fully human.
This is the place where we live.
There is no other place than this for us.
Being fully human is our mission,
our goal,
our created purpose.

What fools we are!
If we would only allow the silence
to well up around us,
we would discover God there,
blessing us for who we are,
not scolding us for failing to be divine!

We would find at our center,
present there as promised,
only beauty, not ugliness
only goodness, not evil,
only light, never darkness.

For,
if we could summon the courage
to make that journey of grace,
we would find God there,
living in our Hearts.

God is not in heaven,
God is Here.

But,
you protest,
and rightly so,
"How can we hear God?
How does God answer us in prayer?"

A fair question.
God, Rahner has pointed out,
does not speak many "words" to us.
Rather,
God speaks a single Word
in the one who prays.
That Word,
filled with grace and truth,
that divine Word,
is nothing less than the life of the one who prays.
That life,
seen now from the point of view of God,
is a life ever more oriented to Mystery,
ever more open to the Holy,
ever more fully Human.
God's answer to our prayer is our very life.
We are revealed to ourselves,
empowered to live,
and readied for work.
Love is not a feeling,
it is a commitment,
and this is God's unconditional commitment,
which is unconditional love,
for us.

So the Word God speaks is Us.
But in order to hear this Word,
    we must silence ourselves,
    our screaming hearts,
    and make room there for this Word to echo.
Silence of the heart
    will lead us to this Mystery.
       (The word "mystery"
       comes from a Greek word
       meaning "to keep silence.")
But,
because this silencing of our hearts
    requires a death-to-self
    which is frightening for us,
    which appears lonely for us,
    and which will inevitably
    lead us to uncertain places,
that Word spoken by God which is us
also has the power to cause us to take flight
    and to take refuge
    in the safer realm
       of Everybody
          or Everything.
But when we pray the prayer of grace,
    and we resist this urge to take flight,
    we can allow the Word
    spoken in silence
    by God who loves us
    to take deep root in us.
Then we are not Everybody,
    which is really nobody in particular,
    but rather then we can become Somebody!

Then we can contemplate the loveliness
    of this most Holy Mystery
    and our journey inward
    will bring us to rest.

"Be still and know that I am God."

9

TEACHING GRACE TO OTHERS

O nce we have become convinced
that noticing
and living with grace
is important to us,
we will want to share that with others.

We're going to talk about that next
by sharing one of the great stories
of the Christian Scriptures.

This is the story of Philip,
one of the people called by Jesus.
Now,
I know that
Jesus invited quite a few people
to follow him.
We want to take a minute now
to step back and consider
how he did this calling.

We often hear these stories about
how the disciples and apostles
were called by Jesus.
But I'm not sure that we always
understand them well.

There are a lot of details
about the life of Jesus
that have been lost to history.
We aren't sure where or what he did
on a day-to-day basis.
Those personal facts really aren't important.
At least,
they weren't to the early
followers of Jesus
who were the ones who wrote the stories down.
But there are some things that
we can surely surmise about his life
and his way of being with others.
We take these surmisings from the whole gospel:
We read the text and we can say,
based on what was finally included,
that Jesus was this sort of person
or that sort.
We are fully able
to draw some conclusions there
about what was behind the stories
that were written down.
What was behind them,
their context,
is really very important
because it helps us know
what the writers meant to say.

For example,
we probably wouldn't conclude,
from what is written there,
that Jesus was given to much violence.
There just isn't anything in the text
to support that.
Nor would we say that he was insensitive to others.
He seemed,
in fact,
to be very sensitive:
weeping, caring, noticing.

We could conclude,
    it seems to me,
    from what we see in the text,
    that Jesus had a very inclusive approach
        to his friendships
        as well as to the Kingdom of God.
There are other conclusions we could reach,
    and some we could surmise,
but we really do not know any of this for sure.

Nevertheless,
    surmising is enough,
    and it is a valid way
    to try to understand more deeply
    the life and times
of Jesus of Nazareth.

Furthermore,
    many of the stories that we have about Jesus
    are summaries of much more
    that must have gone on.
I mean,
    the entire text of the gospels
    can be read in less than a few hours
    but it summarizes many years
    in the life of a very active man.
It is helpful for us,
    within limits,
    to consider what each story
        is meant to tell us
    by considering
        what the story summarizes
        in the life of Jesus
and the men and women who were with him.
For example,
    Jesus heals someone.
On the face of it,
    that seems pretty simple.
        But is it?

Those healing stories
    can tell us a great deal about
    Jesus and his friends.
They are not the stories
    of a first-century magician
    walking down country roads
    zapping people with healing,
        waving his hand like a wand
and stirring up the evil spirits of the day.

No.
They are much richer than that.
They summarize a relationship between Jesus
    and the women and men who were healed.

A relationship:
    The gospel is about relationships,
    healed and healing relationships.
Who knows what must have gone on
    between Jesus and those
    seeking healing in his presence?
Who can guess the depth of
    compassion and care
    that he must have shown to them?
Time and again,
    when everyone else had given up on someone,
    or condemned them,
        Jesus was the one
        brave enough and big enough
        to stay with them
            and offer them friendship.
First it was this woman,
    then that man.
Then he would take on the crowd
    in defense of a so-called public sinner.
Soon he would turn up here healing this one,
    then he would show up there healing that one.
The only ones he did not bother
    to defend
    were the self-righteous.

He must have figured that they
and their judgmental attitudes
could defend themselves.

Who would Jesus defend today?
I'm pretty sure he would be with those
caught in the nightmare of divorce.
Healing relationships was one of his specialities.
And I can't imagine that he would be absent
from those persecuted
for honestly trying to live out their
sexual orientations
even when those orientations are not the norm.
I would think we would find him
holding out against those
who continue to batter and brutalize women,
whether physically or economically.
Prostitution is still around;
I think he'd continue to be with them.
But I think he'd concentrate more today
on the religious self-righteous,
especially those
who have taken it on themselves
to condemn others. He would,
I think,
ask them the same question:
"Which of you is without this sin?"

There are others,
many others,
whom Jesus would likely defend or confront today.
We live in a much more complex world,
much more militarized
much more psychologized
much more mobile, rapid, and linked.
It is much more complex,
but Jesus would sort it out,
as he did the world of the first century,
and hold it accountable
to his central question:

Does this build or destroy relationships?
Is this unilateral,
    or is it relational?

Sorting it out this way
    is what we must do.

Our God is a God of love,
    a God of commitment,
    of care for us,
    of unconditionality,
    of relationship with us.

What happened in the Genesis story about the Garden
    and the people who lived there
    is a story about relationships, too.
But in the Garden,
    our relationships were not healed,
        they were ruptured.
There the people,
    the man and the woman,
    were ruptured from each other
        as much as they were from God.

The story tells us
    that their nakedness,
    which had been a lovely part
        of their life together,
now became a cause of shame for them.
They had had nothing to hide,
    but now there were secrets between them.
The one mind and one heart
    that they had felt and lived with
    were now no longer one,
        they were divided,
        ruptured,
        ruined,
        and destroyed.

This is our story, you see,
   told about someone else.
The story of Genesis is true, literally true,
   but it is true about us,
   not about them.
That's the point of the writer.

So then Jesus,
   eventually naked again on the cross,
   restored that oneness
   through that act of forgiveness
      which he provided there.
We have already talked about this,
but we should emphasize something important again:
   the oneness and wholeness
   of life in harmony
   and relationship,
      once known in the Garden,
      was replaced there with
         division
         distrust
         illness
         and pain.
In a word, life became death.

We must never forget that the physical illness,
   often healed by Jesus,
   did not exist until this rupture
   between the man and the woman in the Garden.
So in healing illness and blindness,
   Jesus was really healing relationships.
   We know this is true
because the entire context of the gospels
         suggests it.
The gospel offers us a chance
   to return to
         unity
         trust
         wholeness
         and pleasure.
In the Word, death becomes life.

It is never very helpful for us
    to use a single line
    of the Scriptures
    to try to prove this point
        or that.
Yet certain people
    frequently do this.
They want to show that this act
    or that one
    is sinful,
    as though Jesus would have said so
        if he were here.
Or else they want to take certain specific
    lines of the gospel as literal,
    in order to serve their purpose,
        while they willy-nilly
        ignore others.
This is a-la-carte scriptural literalism
    and it doesn't fly very well.

Rather,
    we should try to look
    at the whole gospel
    to understand what Jesus would
    teach in our day.

Story after story in the gospel
    remind us that Jesus was a person of love.
His own words,
    and the words attributed to him later
    by those who knew him,
    are filled with appeals to love others.
So, when the gospel tells us
    that someone who encountered Jesus
    was healed,
        the gospel is summarizing
        a friendship.
It is summarizing a way that Jesus
    related to this person,
    a way he had of loving them
    and of being loved by them.

Jesus meant not only to teach us of God's love
　　but also to show us that
　　we are capable of that depth of love, too.
So we must conclude that,
　　while Jesus loved and healed in his day,
　　he was also loved by others,
　　　　and was healed by them as well.
In short,
the healing and loving of Jesus and his friends
　　was a two-way street.
Don't forget
　　that Jesus was fully human
and as much in need of love as we are!

Well,
　　getting back to Philip,
　　the same is true there.
When Jesus called Philip,
　　he didn't just walk by him,
　　glancing sort of sideways at him
　　and say,
　　　　"Follow me."
Heavens no.
The call of Philip
　　must have been the culmination
　　of a long,
　　　　maybe life-long friendship,
　　　　or at least of a steady relationship
　　that allowed Philip to see Jesus plainly
　　and Jesus to see Philip plainly.

"I call you friends,"
Jesus once told his closest followers,
　　"because I have revealed myself
　　entirely to you."
Does that sound like something
　　that could happen in a mere moment?

With Peter, James, and John,
　　the fishermen,

it may have been even more.
Jesus loved the sea.
In some of the gospel accounts
    we find story after story
    of him crossing over the lake,
    teaching from a boat,
    spending time on the beach.
As an adult,
    Jesus probably lived in Capernaum
    which is a small town
    located on the Sea of Galilee.
He may have lived just up the street
    from the beach,
    and he was probably a merchant there.
We would guess that his trade
    may have been woodworking
    since we understand
that his folks were in that business.

But try not to think of him
    as God living on your block.
Think of him as just another person
    living there,
because that is just what he was.

So there he lived,
    and we know that he loved the beach front
    so we can easily surmise
    that he would have spent quite a bit of time
        down there,
        watching the fishermen work,
        watching the boats come and go,
        keeping an eye on the weather a bit,
        and getting to know the workers.
They were probably his closest friends, these guys.
They were his buddies.
They sort of grew up together,
    got to know each other
    got to trust each other
    and got to love each other.

There is a kind of unplanned friendship
that just sneaks up on you.
You see these people every day,
or very frequently,
and then one day you suddenly realize
that you really do love them.
You realize that this is
the kind of friend
about whom you say,
"He's really a great friend;
there's something really special
about him!"
Or,
"She's the best friend anyone could ask for!"
That probably pretty well describes
Jesus and these folks.
What they did together
was they related together:
they talked,
explored the truth in their lives,
exposed the shame,
and learned to love.
It was for all of them,
including Jesus,
a powerful
irresistible
love:
a deep, profound love,
a falling in love,
a being in love,
a friendship.
It began on this beach,
and later,
it would take a dramatic turn
on this same beach
at a breakfast fish-fry
that changed the world.

Jesus and these people did eventually
   make a more formal pact to be together,
   but the agreement was mutual:
   we know this from the way God has acted
   in the whole Bible.
It was mutual:
   Jesus promised to remain with them
   and they promised to remain with Jesus.

So when Jesus called these guys
   or any of the other
   men or women
   who were in his company,
he called them in the context of love.
He called them to himself
   and to each other
   and they also called him!
They called him to themselves.
And in this mutuality
   they all found peace,
      comfort,
      strength,
      wholeness,
      and holiness.

There were others he called:
   men and women whom he'd met
   or lived near
or gotten to know over the years.
They formed a little company of friends,
   a community of searchers
   and believers.

How do we know that Jesus
   and the men and women who joined him
   were such good friends?
We know because we have read
   some of the speeches that Jesus made
   about life and love
   and we have read some of the prayers
      that he prayed.

All of them,
    the speeches and the prayers,
    all point to one thing:
        the central point of the gospel is Love,
        God's and Ours.
Does it seem reasonable, then,
    that Jesus,
    who proclaimed this message,
    would have been someone in love himself?
Does it seem reasonable, too,
    that the ones called to be with him
    would have been in love with him
    and he with them?
Yes, I think it does; it definitely does seem
reasonable that that would have been true.

This has all been an introduction
    to our thoughts about teaching grace.
It has been an introduction
    but, in a way,
    it has also been the whole story
    about teaching grace to others.

In a word,
you don't teach grace to others.
    Grace can only be shared,
        only shared in love,
        in the context of a loving friendship.
We don't like to hear this
    because we know how impractical it is.

We live in a world of efficiency.
    Numbers mean everything.
We are in the habit of mass-producing Christians.
We have huge confirmation classes
    and gigantic first communion classes.
We make sure everyone gets there,
    everyone: ready or not.
So this business of sharing grace through love
    is very impractical indeed.
It takes a lot of time to love.

And it certainly would tend to do in
  the notion that a single person
  could ever be pastor
  to more than about ten or a dozen others,
    ten or a dozen at the most.

It also completely dismantles
  any hierarchical approach
  to ministry
and it introduces the circular
  as a norm.

But have you ever wondered about this:
    If Jesus had such great power to heal,
    why didn't he just zap the whole world
        before he died
        and make it all well?
Why did he deal with so few people
    during his lifetime?
I mean,
    it seems that he really had a chance
    and he blew it.

But did he?
We've been looking at his life here
    from the point of view of grace
    and we've found that he healed
    loved
    cried
    cared
    lived and died
only in relationship to others.
He lived out a model for us.
    He didn't just "zap" the world
because he knew he had to love the world.
You don't love someone
    by zapping them,
    whether with a sacrament
    a blessing
    or your leadership.

But we are so intent on full churches
　　that we often don't see
the chance we really have
　　　to do as Jesus did.
Rather than meeting one another
　　in the friendship of Jesus,
　　we meet each other
in the parish schedule somewhere.

We are seriously concerned about those who
　　do not attend our churches any longer.
We wonder why they've left us,
　　where they've gone,
　　why they no longer listen to us.
But I think *we* should listen to *them.*
For many of them,
　　they were making a very honest choice
　　not to continue to live
　　in a church
　　that refused to be
　　　at least as inclusive as Jesus
　　　would have been.

If there is a danger for modern Christianity,
　　it is probably full churches.

I don't think we can understand this fully
　　without talking now
　　about the Edict of Milan.

You're probably thinking that I've lost my mind.
"What could the Edict of Milan,
　　whatever that is,
　　have to do with teaching grace to others?"

If there is such a thing as a "non-feast"
　　then I nominate the Edict of Milan
　　　for that day.
It was a dark day for grace.

Sometime about 300 years after the death of Jesus
and the birth of the family that followed him
a power-hungry ruler in Europe
forced everyone living in his realm
to become a Christian or die.
It was sort of reverse martyrdom.
This forced membership in the church
did more harm than good for grace.
(We haven't honored
those who died as "martyrs"
during this time
for honestly refusing to
become Christians.)

There were probably other abuses in the church
at this time,
but the effect of this edict
was to institutionalize something:
Life in Christ,
which is better experienced as a movement.
As a movement,
the followers of Christ
could be alive!
They could share experiences and insights
without reference to a static
organization.
"The Spirit of God," Jesus once remarked,
"blows where it wants. . . ."

But once the church was institutionalized,
the free-flowing grace of God
began to be "dispensed"
through the sacramental system
of a hierarchially dominated organization.
We began then to teach about
the truths of our faith
in systematic ways,
ways that kept the believers in line
dogmatically and morally.

Among the truths we began to teach about
    after the Edict of Milan
    and its accompanying abuses
        was grace.
We defined it,
    catalogued it,
    and dispensed it at will,
        like cigarettes
        from a vending machine.
What a horrible day it was for God's grace.

And ever since that time,
    when Christians go to worship
    many of them are there
    to get a "shot" of religion.
When you get a flu shot,
    you receive just enough of the virus
    to help you build
    a solid resistance to
    anything more profound
        in the way of a flu.
Sunday Mass has the same effect
    for many.
People get just enough "church"
    that they build a resistance
    to anything more profound
        in the way of grace.
This vaccine approach
    to the Eucharist
    results from our over-concentration
    on numbers,
    which began with the Edict of Milan.

But that is all changing now.
We have freed grace from the bonds of death
    and it is alive and well today.
We have learned not to corner
    or control it any longer.

We can help one another to become aware
of what is going on within us,
of how God is acting in our lives
or our world,
but we cannot create that activity.
As such,
grace is discovered from the inside out,
rather than from the outside in.
People become aware of their experience of life,
they become willing to see it,
admit it,
tell the truth about it,
and love it,
and then there is the chance
that they can also
become aware
of the hand of God in that.
But it is not possible
to begin by creating the moment of grace.
Experience just happens.
It cannot be programed or scheduled.
But it can be reflected upon,
which is what will bring us
to recognize the presence of God
and become all that we can be.

So,
while we cannot create grace,
or dispense it,
we can point it out to others.
The most effective way to do that
is to start by
telling the story of your own life,
laying it alongside
the story of God's life.

When we want to teach about grace,
we tend to start by talking about God.
But really,
we would be better off if we began

by talking about ourselves:
    our experiences
    our failures
    our loves
    our hearts.
Remember what we said earlier here,
    that grace is the power
    which leads us to become
    all that we are created to be.
Its purpose is not to make us
    equal with God.
Jesus himself
    did not deem equality with God
    something to be grasped at.
Rather,
    he accepted his full humanity
    and became,
    without anything lacking,
        the person he was created to be.
In that sense,
    Jesus was full of grace and power.

Our first assumption,
    then,
    if we are to teach grace to another person,
    is that God is already active
        in that person's life.
The most we can do
    is to make that person aware of that.
And more,
    God is present there
    offering peace
    life
    breath
    and future
        to that person.
If God were not present to us,
we would not go on being another moment.

The very engine that runs us,
    the generator in our depths:
    that is God.
This generator constantly creates us,
    generates us,
    with a powerful energy.
Paul gives us insight into this
    in the early part of Colossians
    where he gives a summary of
    his view of who Christ is:
"Christ is the energy
    that holds the universe together."

When we live, empowered by the Risen Christ,
    then everything holds together,
    and without Christ we can do nothing.

So we must understand
    that we do not make God present.
God *is* present.
Period.

The most we can do
    is to make this presence known.
And taking our example from Jesus himself,
    that can be done only in the context
    of friendship and love.

So religion classes for young people
    might be a bad idea.
Pouring information about God into peoples' heads,
    as we would pour syrup on pancakes,
    makes no sense whatever.
If you want to train a young person in faith,
    then provide the context for that person
    in which he or she
    can become
        the full person each was created to be.
We must take seriously
    the need to help adults parent their children
    well and kindly,

because in that family context
can be found the first and best
opportunity for real formation
for a young person.

We don't need to teach young people
about religion first.
We need to help them discover themselves.
For to discover themselves,
their profound abilities,
their tremendous potentials,
their personal attributes,
their sexual selves,
their deep insights,
is to discover God within.

This self-discovery
is really a way to become attuned
to the revelation of God
as it is going on around us.
God is our creator,
our generator,
our source of energy and life.
God reveals God-self to us
in Jesus Christ who is
our empowerment,
our revealer,
our source of selfhood.
God's revelation happens, we know,
only when a Spirit of Friendship happens
between us
which gives us
our courage,
our sharing,
our source of love.

For all of us,
young and old,
the only real way
to recognize and accept grace
is to be formed in it.
Being formed will happen over time,
time of personal prayer,
small group sharing,

community-wide celebrations,
study of Scripture,
theological reflection,
and spiritual friendship.

We badly need formation programs
for all the adults
of the church,
a similar kind of formation
that members of religious communities have had
since earlier in this century.
We really do not learn grace
as much as we are formed in it.
But what we need first
is a willingness to Pause in our busy-ness,
Pause to reflect on what is happening
in our lives
and our days.
Without this willingness to Pause,
all the formation programs in the world
will not help us recognize God's hand
in our lives.
We must learn to take the time
and the quieting of our hearts
that will make this Holy Pause possible for us.

We should pause in the morning,
at noontime,
at suppertime,
and before bedtime.

If we have become aware in these times of Pausing
of the Holy One in our midst;
If we have become filled with awareness of grace
within us and around us,
then teaching grace to others
will not be difficult:
Others will be with us
and come away knowing that they have
found in us what they seek for themselves.

10

GRACE AND THE CHURCH

O ver the years,
the church has been called
the depository of grace
and it has taken on itself
the role of dispensing grace
to the faithful.

We need to talk about this now
because for most of us
our dependency on the church handling grace
for us
must now be transformed
into our own call to be people of grace
for ourselves
but especially for each other.

We should begin by talking about
the church itself.
In order to properly understand
what church is all about
we need to turn around the ways
that we have traditionally looked at
the reality of the
assembling of the followers of Christ.

We are in the habit,
    long learned and well remembered,
    of thinking about the church
    from the "top" down.
When we write the histories of our parishes
    we usually begin by
    listing the various pastors
    who have been in charge there
        over the years.
The history of the church universal
    is given as the list of the popes
    and their places in history.
We generally begin from what we perceive
    the top to be:
    the ones in charge:
        the priests, bishops, religious.

We have to stop doing that.

According to the theology of Vatican II,
    those in charge are to be servants
    of the rest.
They should be considered the least,
    the "bottom,"
    if you will.
The official church is the People of God,
    and the officials of the church
    are to be servants to the rest.
When we write the history of the church,
    we should begin with its official members,
    the People of God.

This popular saying,
    first uttered officially at
    the Second Vatican Council,
    that the church is the People of God,
        is very important to us today.
It's a very interesting saying,
    and one that,
    if we ever dare to take it seriously,
can change our lives completely.

Who are these "People of God"?
A crucial question if we are to understand
   how grace and the church relate.
The people of God,
   first of all,
   are not simply those who show up
   for Mass on Sunday.

People do not live in their churches.
They live in their homes.
People live in "secular" communities,
   otherwise known as
   circles of families and friends.
Everyone lives in some sort of circle of people.
A few people have absolutely no one,
   but almost everyone has someone,
   even if that someone is not terribly close
      or available
      or regular
      or faithful.
People live with others.
For the most part,
   we do not organize these circles
   around the church.
We don't schedule our meetings in the
   local parish bulletin.
Rather,
   we simply gather with each other,
   no big deals,
      we just get together.
You know,
   there's a weekend coming
   and one of us calls another
   and suggests that maybe we should get together
      for a movie
      or dinner
      or to go to the lake
      or a ball game
      or just to visit.

Or maybe we just drop in on each other.
    Or we call each other for help
    because maybe we're moving
    or building
    or painting
    or hauling things.
Sometimes its a birthday
    or an anniversary
    or a wedding
    or a baptism
    or funeral.
We're neighbors and friends;
    we're family.
Everyone lives in a circle of people
    and,
    if you thought about it
    even for a minute,
        you could make a list of the
        people in your circle.

Now its important to realize
    that not all the bonds in this circle
    are the same.
Some are very deep bonds,
    some very shallow.
Some people are new to us,
    but they're still in our circle.
Some people in our circle have been around
    for a long time in our lives:
    they go way back.
Others seem to enter for a while,
    hang out with our gang,
    but then circumstances or situations change
    and they're gone.
We might even ask about them later,
    "Have you seen so and so lately?"
        or
    "Whatever happened to what's-her-name?"

These circles are fluid,
    dynamic,
    changing,
    and organic.
They ebb and flow,
    sometimes gathering often,
    sometimes not often enough, it seems.
We might gather often during the holidays,
    but maybe less often in February.
But then they may meet more often later in the spring,
    or there may be a reunion
    of some kind.

Not everyone in these circles relates the same.
    To some you may feel very close,
    say, to a spouse
    or children
    or special friends.
To others you may be a bit more distant,
    but those people would be
    closer to others,
    and to some that you don't even know.
In a sense,
    each person's circle
    is personal.
Each of us is the center of our circle.
We live in the midst
    of an organic network of relationships.

These circles,
    these organic networks
    of family, friends, strangers, and neighbors,
    these are the People of God
    and it's this People of God
    that Vatican II was talking about
        when it defined the church.
We meet usually,
    in homes,
    businesses,
    bars,
    and cafes: these are our buildings,
        our places.

We meet where we are comfortable,
where we feel acceptance,
where we know the folks will welcome us,
where we know we belong.

That's it:
we meet where we know we belong.

Our purpose in meeting
is to continue our lives.
This doesn't seem like a big deal to us
and it really isn't.
It's a great reason to get together
and we generally can't wait
to get together again.
We meet to continue our lives,
to get through this day
and on to the next.
We talk about what's happening now
and what's happening next.
We compare notes on life,
naturally sharing,
naturally telling the stories of our lives.

Sometimes church leaders want to get
people into small groups
in order to encourage them to "share."
Most people resist this,
it seems a bit artificial,
a bit forced,
a bit foreign to us.
What we must realize
is that sharing is natural to being human.
People do it all the time.
They do it in their natural circles.
The church can no more organize it
than it can dispense grace.

The very most the church can do is to enhance
    the sharing
    by teaching folks that what they do
    in their everyday lives
    is sacred and holy.

This doesn't mean bringing them
    to the church building
    to do it there.
It means legitimating
    and recognizing what happens
    in homes
    and bars
    and restaurants
and other gathering places.

In a word,
the church should bless people's lives,
    teach them to recognize the holy there,
    and then get out of the way.

Grace,
    like the Spirit,
        blows where it wants.

So these are the people we're talking about,
    and this is where they naturally gather,
    and why,
    and how.

The implications of this understanding
    of the church and how it meets
    are many and important
    to us today.
There are many questions we must ask.

If what happens with coffee and cookies
    over the kitchen table
    when friends or family gather there
    is not eucharistic,

then can what happens in church on Sunday
truly be considered Eucharist?

If what happens when friends or family
gather with beer and pretzels
to celebrate their lives
is not eucharistic,
then how can those same people
gather to celebrate on the weekend?

If the parent and child who make up
after fighting over spilled milk
do not celebrate reconciliation together,
then can what happens in the
reconciliation room at church
mean anything?

If the family gathers to pray with a sick member
and what happens in that bedside moment
is not sacramental,
then how can a priest
make any difference there?

If two people in love
haven't come to the point in their friendship
where their devotion to each other
has not produced a marriage
between them,
then how can a sacramental wedding create
such a marriage?

If the leadership we need,
even for public prayer,
seems to come
from married persons
or women
and if the community of the faithful
calls these persons
as well as celibate males,
then how long can we hold out
against this New Spirit?

These questions haunt us today
    as we seek to live our lives in the church.
But therein lies the point:
    We used to say that we live in the world
    and we go to church for Mass,
but today we say that we live in the church
    and we go out to the world
    to offer healing and forgiveness
        there.
We have begun a re-examination today
    of how grace is offered and experienced
in the liturgies and sacraments of the church.
The results of this re-examination
    seem likely to be profound!

Also by Bill Huebsch...

A Radical* Guide for Catholics
rooted in the essentials of our faith

This is truly a handbook for the contemporary Catholic. Taking its cue from the word "radical," the book spells out a vision of Christianity related not to ideology, but to lived reality. It speaks to the heart about the matters of everyday life: marriage, families, love, money, greed, prayer and conscience. Each chapter of the book offers two ways to develop our call to be Catholic—"Reflections," which offer guidance on conscience formation, and "LifeSongs," which are the stories of human experience that give flesh and blood to the book. Like some of Huebsch's previous books, *A Radical* Guide for Catholics* is written in sense-line style, which adds a warmth and familiarity to the topics presented.
ISBN: 0-89622-525-9, 224 pages, $9.95 (order C-84)

A New Look at Prayer
Searching for Bliss

Spiritually rich, theologically exciting and written in an appealing sense-line style, *A New Look at Prayer* is ideal both for newcomers to prayer and for those wishing to explore and expand their existing prayer life. Readers will find a guide for listening to God, for discerning and discovering both who they are and who they can be. Helpful questions for reflection end each chapter and are useful for study group discussion or individual consideration.
ISBN: 0-89622-458-9, 128 pages, $7.95 (order C-45)

Rethinking Sacraments
Holy Moments in Daily Living

Bill Huebsch has looked long and hard at the changes brought about by Vatican II. He has come up with a redefining, a refinement, of what it's like to experience sacrament today—that sacrament is Christian service, grace lived out in our daily lives. Throughout the pages of this book, readers find words to challenge them, to address old ideas and nurture new ones on what sacrament now means to Catholics. The book offers new paths to arrive at the holy moments in our everyday experience.
ISBN: 0-89622-393-0, 194 pages, $7.95 (order W-90)

Available at religious bookstores or from
TWENTY-THIRD PUBLICATIONS
P.O. Box 180 • Mystic, CT 06355 • **1-800-321-0411**